"There is no better guide to Teresa of Avila's spirituality than Tessa Bielecki who has spent nearly fifty years engaging with this earthy mystic and translating her teachings into sensible lessons for all of us. This amazing book is a testament to Tessa's deep love for, and kinship with, Teresa. The accessibility of Tessa's language makes Teresa's life and work—her very being—relevant to those of us who want to answer the impulse to live a life that is both deeply human and holy. As a young mother of two very small children, I especially appreciate Tessa's ability to distill the wisdom and beauty of this saint into practical ways of having a 'willing response to whatever life requires of us' so that we may let 'life itself become our asceticism'. Tessa helps us to see ourselves in Teresa—no matter our life circumstances—as we seek intimacy with the Divine."

— V. K. Harber, co-founder, Samdhana-Karana Yoga: A Healing Arts Center

"Tessa Bielecki has intuited the spirit of St. Teresa of Avila. She looks like her, thinks and loves like her, and lives like her. *This book on St. Teresa is a gem.* Study alone—and how assiduously Tessa did that—would not issue in such a pertinent and perfect reflection on this exquisite woman. Intimate union between these two great Teresas is the only explanation."

— William McNamara, founder of *Spiritual Life* magazine and The Spiritual Life Institute

"Tessa has the rare gift of being able to transmit the teachings of a sixteenth-century Christian mystic with such clarity and passion that they address our contemporary spiritual needs with startling relevance. Tessa's deep intimacy with Teresa of Avila permeates this beautiful book and creates an invitational space for readers of any tradition (or none) to enter into their own transformational relationship with the 'wild woman of Avila.'"

— MIRABAI STARR, TRANSLATOR OF ST. TERESA'S *THE INTERIOR CASTLE* AND *THE BOOK OF MY LIFE,* AUTHOR OF *CARAVAN OF NO DESPAIR* AND *GOD OF LOVE*

"Tessa Bielecki is a devoted contemplative hermit and a fiery and outspoken leader in Christian-Buddhist dialogue. Writing about St. Teresa, she has gone far beyond simple biography to create a powerful contemporary teaching on Catholic mysticism for the general public. She has also written a book which speaks to Western Buddhists and others seeking common ground for Christian and Buddhist traditions. Spiritual practitioners of all faiths will find this simple book a rich treasury of human experience which can be read again and again as a continuing inspiration to living a life of service to others."

— MARK SANDO MININBERG, MOUNTAINS AND RIVERS ZEN BUDDHIST ORDER

"This is a good, lively, even exciting presentation of St. Teresa's vision. Even the expert in Teresian spirituality will find much here. The book is a welcome relief, fresh, challenging you to drink deeply at the springs of the Spirit; to fill your lungs with crisp mountain air; to live life fully and deliberately. Its centerpiece is the call to spousal prayer, following in the tradition of The Song of Songs. By using the strong language of human romance and sexuality, Tessa brings out the possibilities for intimacy with God in startling relief."

— FRED BITTLE, *CAELUM ET TERRA*

"*Holy Daring* is infectious and opens the heart to a larger and more luscious possibility. Like St. Teresa, Tessa approaches her Divine Beloved as husband, friend and lover in all its intimate and erotic forms. For both women, living some 400 years apart, spousal prayer means life lived to the fullest— far from the image of crusty, cloistered renunciation of the world. This book clearly applies to anyone embarked on a disciplined spiritual path. Its succinctly divided segments address several roadblocks to realization with the Divine. It is refreshingly personal, not only the writings of St. Teresa, but also Tessa's own testimony of faith. One begins to feel understood from the inside out when coming upon some detail perplexing in one's own practice."

— *MUDRA'S TOO SENSE*, PRESCOTT, AZ

"This fresh, upbeat, and deftly profound book joyfully reconnects the fullness of our lives and the depth of our prayer. It rekindles something of St. Teresa of Avila's outrageous spiritual impulse for contemporary readers."

— THE TATTERED COVER, DENVER, CO

"I almost devoured my review copy of *Holy Daring* and feel energized and renewed."

— BOB HAMMA, SPIRITUAL BOOK ASSOCIATES

"In the midst of reading many highly academic articles on St. Teresa, it's been refreshing to read a work like Tessa's: informative, yet so deeply human and so clearly full of love for Teresa."

— MICHAEL O'MALLEY, NORRISTOWN, PA

"*Holy Daring* is exciting my heart and soul. Tessa's advice is simple but electrifying! I want to shout with joy. Think of it: 'I look at him, as he looks at me.'"

— JESSICA DANSON, SEDONA, AZ

HOLY DARING

HOLY DARING

*The Earthy Mysticism of St.
Teresa, the Wild Woman of Avila*

TESSA BIELECKI

Foreword by
Adam Bucko

Adam Kadmon Books
Rhinebeck, New York

"The old shall be renewed,
and the new shall be made holy."
— Rabbi Avraham Yitzhak Kook

ISBN: 978-1-939681-59-1
eBook ISBN: 978-1-939681-60-7

Adam Kadmon Books is a joint imprint of Monkfish Book Publishing Company and Albion-Andalus Books
22 East Market Street, Suite 304
Rhinebeck, New York 12572
(845) 876-4861
www.monkfishpublishing.com
www..albionandalus.com

For Adam Bucko, Rory McEntee,
Netanel Miles-Yépez, and all "New Monastics"
who strive to live a life of contemplation
and sacred activism in the world.

CONTENTS

Foreword

IT IS AN HONOR to write the Foreword to this important book on the spirituality of the Wild Woman of Avila.

I originally came across the author of this book in 1995. I was a young emigré, studying theology, spending my summers at a monastery, and trying to live the ascetical path of emptying and detachment in the urban wilderness of New York City. My understanding of detachment at that point in my life was a bit misguided. I practiced what can more accurately be called disengagement and, as a result, spent years separated from feelings, my self, and ultimately life itself.

One Friday evening, I went to a talk offered by a Carmelite hermit. Walking into the venue, I spotted her, dressed in her Carmelite habit. The space was immediately infused with aliveness. In her I could feel a deep prayerfulness that was wild and earthy, completely different from what I was familiar with. She was there not to deny life but to maximize it and turn into something worth living.

Her name was Tessa Bielecki, and that night she talked about St. Teresa of Avila. It became immediately clear that St. Teresa is among Tessa's best friends and an intimate companion. That evening Tessa said something that completely changed my path and my life. She said that "falling in love with life is the first step on the mystical path." I remember hearing those words and feeling confused. My ascetical discipline had not led to a love of life. In fact, I wasn't even really alive.

It took me many years to unpack exactly what Tessa meant. Her work took me from a desire to find God in the silence of the Himalayas to finding God in the broken bodies of children living on the streets of New York City. Ultimately, that statement called me from a detached and disengaged state back into life: life that calls us to demanding and "generous, self-spending service," life that asks us to be who we were born to be and offer that in service of God's dream of compassion, non-violence and justice.

The book that you hold in your hands is truly extraordinary. The woman who wrote it is the best guide I know to the beauty and wildness that is the earthy and mystical St. Teresa of Avila. After living 50 years as a hermit-monk, building monasteries in three different countries, and, not unlike St. Teresa, developing a new format for a more feminine form of monasticism, Tessa still continues to speak to us from her desert hermitage where she now lives as a lay hermit, sharing the gift of her life-long friendship with St. Teresa with all of us.

At a time when patriarchal models of unhealthy disengaged spirituality are failing to equip us with tools for life in a world dominated by ecological and economic injustice, this book does just that. It will help us all discover our true aliveness in God and offer it in service of a world awaiting our caring response.

May the words of this book become your prayer. May you pause often while reading it and delight in the gift being shared with you. May you develop a new friendship with St. Teresa and be changed by it. May you begin to live with holy audacity and holy daring!

— ADAM BUCKO,
New York, New York

PREFACE TO
THE NEW EDITION

S T. TERESA OF AVILA was born on March 28, 1515 and is now over 500 years old. I was given her name at birth but did not "meet" her until the 1970s when I had just turned thirty. I was stunned at how contemporary she was. I felt closer to her than I did to any other woman "friend" and strongly identified with her in almost every way. She was an outgoing personality, a bridal mystic, and a "foundress," traveling around the country creating new contemplative communities.

I wrote the first of my three books about Teresa in the early 1990s when I was about to turn fifty. My personal working title for that study was "The Woman and the Dream." I've long been fascinated by Don Quixote, the "Man from La Mancha," who dreamed the "Impossible Dream," and I saw Teresa struggling with her own dream of renewed contemplative life in the world as I, too, struggled with a similar dream.

Crossroad titled the book, *Teresa of Avila: Mystical Writings,* and published it as part of their Spiritual Legacy Series. I pored through two thousand pages of Teresa's prose, poetry, prayers, and letters in a log cabin outside Crestone, Colorado, during a period of luxurious solitude that Teresa seldom experienced in her lifetime, and I seldom had in my own.

In a turn of events that was both splendid and comical, I ended up writing *Holy Daring* within the same year. I do not recommend this to anyone! I wrote deep in the woods of Nova Scotia this time, in circumstances as challenging as Teresa's, snatching moments throughout busy days of administrative and pastoral duties, in the midst of travels, trouble-shooting, hard manual labor, and a crippling back injury, working deep into the night when I should have been sleeping. Teresa's lighting was not much better than the kerosene lamps in my hermitage, which was even named St. Teresa. We both wrote longhand, but Teresa didn't have an assistant with a laptop computer, powered by a boat battery, since we had no electricity in Nova Nada's rugged log cabins.

Researching for both these books twenty years after I first read Teresa, I was once again stunned at how contemporary she was. Today, another twenty years later, I've just turned 70, and I'm stunned yet again by her contemporary relevance. As I prepare this new edition of *Holy Daring* to honor the 500th Anniversary of Teresa's birth, I marvel at the way this remarkable woman continues to "speak" to us with her wit and her wisdom.

Please let Teresa speak to you now in her own "God-language," and me, too? For both of us, "God" is one of the many names of our dear Friend, our Beloved, the Divine Spouse, in the intimate union of contemplative experience. For us, "God" does not connote hierarchy, patriarchy, or any kind of abuse. If it does for you, as it does for so many, please don't let our language hurt you? Simply substitute your own language and "hear" us out?

For those of you unfamiliar with Teresa's *Interior Castle,* please note that this mystical treatise describes the spiritual journey in terms of moving through seven "mansions" of the King's castle, beginning outside in the antechamber and ending in the most intimate central chamber, the Seventh Mansion, which Teresa describes as the highest stage of spiritual growth. She frequently refers to her beloved Spouse as "King," "Lord," and "His Majesty." Many experts on St. Teresa recommend that if we are to read only one of her works, it should be *The Interior Castle.* This does indeed synthesize her finest teachings. But if we begin and end there, we rob ourselves of insights into more of the pain and beauty Teresa suffered en route to the Seventh Mansion. In her *Life* and *Spiritual Testimonies,* we find more detailed evidence of the excruciating refining process we must undergo to find our lives at last distilled into a rare liqueur, exquisitely delicious and divinely intoxicating.

— TESSA BIELECKI
  Crestone, Colorado
  March 28, 2015

Holy Daring

*The Earthly Mysticism of St. Teresa,
the Wild Woman of Avila*

INTRODUCTION
The Wild Woman of Avila

St. Teresa of Avila was vibrant, alive, and thoroughly engaged with the world. She captivated those around her and continues to fascinate us down through the centuries. She was a dynamic personality: wild as a child, wild as she grew from an adolescent into a ravishing young woman, wildest of all as she reached middle age and set out on her quixotic adventures throughout her native Spain.

Teresa was an earth mother and an earthy mystic, a poet and a brilliant administrator, a shrewd politician and a good friend, walking a dangerous tightrope in a delicate balancing act between realism and idealism, common and uncommon sense, making love and making war.

She was stunning to look at: shining black hair, an unusual face, a more "substantial" than slender figure. She was outgoing, cheerful, charming, and scintillating in her conversation. People from all walks of life listened to her: men and women, bishops and mule drivers, theologians and carpenters, lay folk, and the King of Spain himself.

She was a natural leader. As a child, she had an ingenious capacity for inventing new games and playing the starring role: the knight, the fairy godmother, the martyr burned at the stake. "I was strikingly shrewd when it came to mischief," she confessed. She loved to laugh and laughed often. When she did, the people around her laughed, too.

She liked perfume and fine clothes, chivalry, romance, and the color orange. Many men in Avila were in love with her. "Teresa de Ahumada? With her fine mind, shapely legs, and ample dowry," people said, "she'll marry whomever she chooses," rare freedom in an era of arranged marriages.

Teresa was a prolific writer, a great leader, and a teacher of the art of prayer. In 1970, almost four hundred years after her death, she was recognized as the first woman Doctor of the Church. She also stands out as the only woman in the history of the Roman Catholic Church ever to reform a religious order of men.

What does Teresa have to do with us today? Not many of us can be writers, found a school of spirituality, or reform a group of men. Yet Teresa serves as a vital model for the contemplative thrust desperately needed in our broken world today, when more and more people describe themselves as "spiritual, not religious."

Duende

TERESA HAD THAT MYSTERIOUS QUALITY the Spanish call *duende*, characteristic of gypsies, bullfighters, and flamenco dancers. *Duende* is raw, primitive, tempestuous energy, a vulnerability to inspiration burning in the bloodstream. Fiery and wild, *duende* cannot tolerate neat, tidy categories, conventional styles, cramped forms, or limitations of any kind. It makes us ready to struggle heroically for genuine human freedom in every area of our lives.

In the Arab world, when *duende* enters and transfigures any music, dance, or epic poem, the people cry out "Allah! Allah! God! God!" How close this is to the Spanish "¡Ole! ¡Ole!" Perhaps these cries have the same source, since the Moors, a Muslim people of mixed Berber-Arab descent, invaded Spain in 711 and lived there for almost eight hundred years. They were tragically expelled by Ferdinand and Isabella in 1492, less than twenty-five years before Teresa's birth. The Moors not only left behind the magnificent Alhambra, "the red castle," dominating the city of Granada and the Spanish imagination. They bequeathed to Spain, and through this country to the Western world, a rich legacy, which Teresa inherited but never acknowledged.

Duende is usually associated with artists, musicians, dancers, and poets. Teresa was all of these and more, for she was also a *mystic*, that is, *one who knows God by experience.* Full of *duende*, Teresa made mysticism into music, poetry, art, and an ecstatic dance with the Beloved, but not without walking the "royal road" of suffering like every creative genius.

The Movie Version

TERESA'S LIFE WAS SUCH HIGH DRAMA, why not indulge our wildest imagination? See the all-engulfing solitude of the Castilian plain, the ninety stone turrets of the formidable walls of Avila, the sharp jagged peaks of the Gredos Sierra against the skyline. Smell the lush vegetation in the Andalusian courtyards. Hear the musical sounds of Teresa's voice, her tambourine, castanets, and drum, which she played even as a nun. Imagine sitting down with her for a good visit, basking in her wide embrace, her gaiety, and the depth of her wisdom, for Teresa was a woman of character as well as charm.

Visualize her colorful adventures on a movie screen: her Jewish grandfather degraded by the Inquisition, stripped to the waist and paraded through the streets of Toledo in a humiliating procession through the jeering crowds; her five brothers sailing to South America and fighting for the conquest of Peru, Colombia, Argentina, Ecuador, and Chile; her beloved St. John of the Cross, escaping from his nine-month imprisonment with the help of Mary, the Mother of Jesus, and a mongrel dog.

Imagine the beautiful black-eyed Teresa at a party, at prayer or doing penance; laughing over the lizard that crawled up her arm and landed in the face of her friend Antonio Ruiz; or weeping over the sudden death of her friend and brother Lorenzo; talking to workmen as she designed and built monastery after monastery; composing little verses to sing at celebrations; or falling down the stairs and breaking her arm so badly it was useless for the last five years of her life.

Watch her travel back and forth across the Spanish countryside in a rickety covered wagon, joking with her rustic muleteers, or giving astute spiritual guidance to the wealthy merchants who often accompanied her. See her captivating half the men in Spain, including the King, not as a young eligible girl with a good dowry, but as a middle-aged Mother Foundress, *la Madre Fundadora,* who needed help from high places and got it, often at the price of her own pain.

Teresa did not become an integrated human being all at once, any more than we do. Her sanctification was a gradual process that took her entire lifetime. And like us, she made many mistakes, some serious. She knew fear, failure, and human weakness, loneliness, illness, and exhaustion, the joy of sympathy and the pain of misunderstanding. Before she could soar like an eagle, she had to crawl on her belly like a snake, literally, as she slowly began to move again after an excruciating paralysis that lasted three years. Throughout her sufferings, Teresa was humbly and heroically aware of destiny and God's designs, and she clung to these tenaciously. She grew into a giant, a conquistador of the spiritual life, a Doctor of the Church, and a saint for all seasons.

The winsome and sometimes outrageous details about Teresa's life help us fall in love with her. If we fall in love with her, we may fall in love with the God she herself loved so madly. And when we love God this passionately, we love life passionately.

There is an intimate connection between life and prayer. When we really live, fully, exuberantly, and divinely, we inevitably pray. In almost fifty years as a spiritual guide, I have never taught people how to pray. Instead, I've tried to inspire people to live: to set the stage and create the climate for prayer through a "lively human atmosphere" that makes it possible for prayer to erupt naturally and spontaneously.

A lively human atmosphere is not artificial, fragmented, or workaholic, but natural, deliberate, balanced, sacred and poetic. As Jesus said, "I have come so that you may have life and have it to the full." If St. Teresa, the wild woman of Avila, prayed well, it's because she lived well. The first secret we learn from her example, then, is to live life as she did: with passion, "holy daring," and to the hilt!

Holy Daring: Six Conversations

IN *ZEST FOR LIFE*, our first conversation with Teresa, we begin to learn how to create a lively human atmosphere by embracing our human bodies and the body of the earth, celebrating the gifts life gives us, the importance of humor and a vibrant emotional life, which includes the gift of tears and the experience of impermanence.

Our second conversation discusses the *Agony and Ecstasy* of life expressed in the agony and ecstasy of prayer, which Teresa describes in colorful and flamboyant images. She urges us to become earthy mystics and experience "holy sensuousness," and even "holy madness" in our prayer. Teresa teaches a simple kind of contemplative prayer. In her meditations on the two sisters, Martha and Mary, she demonstrates the unity of contemplation and action and helps us "make time" for contemplative practice by "stealing" time.

Our third conversation on *Spousal Prayer* presents Teresa as a "bridal mystic." We look at The Song of Songs, erotic energy, the value of "sublimation" (transforming erotic energy and making it sublime), our choice between mysticism and neurosis, and obstacles to divine intimacy, which include puritanism, promiscuity, "angelism," fear, and an excessive use of reason.

Conversation four on *Love-Wounds and Service* explains how our contemplative prayer inevitably leads to generous, self-spending contemplation-in-action. What does Teresa mean when she calls us not servants but "slaves" in the service of God and the world? Why is the cross such a deep mystery and metaphor for purification of the ego? How can it be both a sword of sorrow and a sword of joy, or a piercing fiery arrow? What does it mean to "long to die and live to serve?"

Meeting the Beloved is our fifth conversation. How do we set the stage for our encounter with the Divine? We look at the classical Christian tradition of *lectio, meditatio, oratio,* and *contemplatio,* with some contemporary twists and earthy meditation practices. Why are "touchstones" important? What about times, places, and postures for prayer? What is "intercession?" How do we know our divine encounter is authentic?

Our sixth conversation celebrates *Fast and Feast.* According to contemporary poet Richard Wilbur, Teresa teaches us to "lock the O of ecstasy within / The tempered consonants of discipline." In this final conversation with Teresa, we look at her "warrior spirit" and how the healthiest asceticism, that is, spiritual "training" or practice, is life itself: natural, organic, and whole. We outline ten spiritual practices especially helpful today: commitment, self-knowledge, accountability, friendship, simplicity, "Rule of Life," vigilance, fasting, solitude, and humility.

Our *Conclusion* is a joyous meditation on paradox and the reconciliation of opposites, "harmony in tension" and *Walking the Tightrope,* my favorite metaphor for the spiritual journey, embodied by high-wire artist, Philippe Petit, and the wild woman of Avila in her ecstatic prayer-poem, "Give me death, give me life."

CONVERSATION ONE
Zest for Life

TERESA TEACHES US how to live the human adventure with zest and enthusiasm. She was in love with every dimension of life: with people and places, music, laughter and celebration, with nature and its abundance.

We see her enthusiasm in the vibrant imagery she draws from her experience of the earth. She speaks of sun and wind and rain, clouds, crystal, and falling comets, tempests, thunderclaps and lightning. She calls God the Sun in the interior of the soul, casting brilliant light into every corner of our being. When she prayed, Teresa loved to look at fields and flowers, "reading" from the book of nature. She loved to live near water, with good soil and gardens. "I should so much like to be among those ducklings of yours," she wrote to her friend Ana in Caravaca.

Teresa urges us to embrace nature in our prayer because nature awakens us, reminding us of the Creator. She can't contain her praise and glorifies God as Lord of the world and Beauty exceeding all other beauties. "Who could make known the majesty with which You reveal Yourself!" she cries out in one of her spontaneous prayers. "O my God, God, God, author of all creation! And what is creation if

You, Lord, should desire to create more? You are almighty; Your works are incomprehensible."

When we have trouble praying, Teresa recommends that we turn to nature: "Go to some place where you can see the sky, and walk up and down a little." Since God is infinite and everywhere, sometimes we rejoice as much in meditating on creation as in meditating on the Divine. Why limit ourselves to only one of creation's mysteries when there are so many? Teresa mentions the mystery of water, the sparrow-hawk, and the tiny ant. Any of these is enough for a whole period of prayer, immersing us in the wonder and wisdom of God. What would happen if we knew "the property of every created thing?"

Since she lived close to the earth, she said the spiritual life is like bees making honey, silkworms spinning their cocoons, fish swimming in a running stream. Depending on our stage of spiritual growth, we may be like mice, toads or snakes, flitting moths, butterflies, doves, wild horses or wounded deer. We may encounter God's majesty as a mighty eagle or a roaring lion.

Teresa's favorite nature image was water. She speaks lavishly of flowing springs, pools, wells, and fountains, rivers, waves, and the sea, urging us to irrigate our hearts with the waters of Life. When instead we clog our lives with triviality and endless distraction, she sees us bogged down in a swamp, struggling to get muddy water out of a puddle.

Teresa also loved fire imagery. If we build a fire in our living room or out in the wilds, we can reflect with her on the raging conflagration which enkindles us with the fire of divine love.

Body-Soul

Teresa was not only in touch with the body of the earth but attuned to the human body, clothed in earth. "We aren't angels," she liked to say, "but we have a body. To desire to be angels while we are on earth... is foolishness." We must always take the body into account, for good or ill.

Teresa keenly intuited the unity of body and soul. Her use of body-soul language clearly indicates a distinction and a difference between the two, but not a dichotomy or separation. In the Christian tradition, the soul never exists as a separate entity. Body and soul belong to one another to such an extent that it is far more appropriate to speak of the "embodied soul" or the "ensouled body."

Teresa describes in detail what may happen to the body during varying stages of prayer. God is not satisfied with the soul but desires the body as well, which shares in our deepest inner experience: "The whole exterior man enjoys this spiritual delight and sweetness." This means we may experience heat or cold, fluidity or rigidity, jubilation or dejection.

We need to understand our bodies and be patient and gentle with them. Our troubles in prayer are often caused by some physical disturbance or even by changes in the weather. Just as the body can be uplifted by sharing in the soul's delightful experience, so the soul can be weighed down and held back by the body's infirmity. So we must sensibly defer, when necessary, to physical weakness, weariness, and sickness. If we force ourselves more during these times, we often "go from bad to worse." We need to take such good care of our bodies that sometimes for health reasons we may have to change the time and length of our prayer or even stop it altogether and instead read, walk or talk to a spiritual companion. "We cannot be at prayer all the time," Teresa wrote her brother Lorenzo. She also continually urged him to stay warm, eat well, and get no less than six hours of sleep at night:

With regard to your sleep, I will tell you—indeed, I will order you—not to take less than six hours. Remember that we middle-aged people need to treat our bodies well so as not to wreck the spirit, which is a terrible trial. You can't think how vexing it has been for me lately: I am afraid to say my prayers or to read, although, as I say, I am better... How silly of you to think that the prayer you are experiencing is the kind that kept me awake! It has nothing to do with it: I was trying far harder to go to sleep than to keep awake.

Teresa's attitude towards the body was basically positive. But she also knew the shadow side. She sometimes felt that her body was an obstacle to her spirit because she had to "waste" so much time taking care of physical needs. This affliction so plagued her that Teresa often wept over the amount of time she had to spend on her health.

She advises us to increase our spiritual capacity for God by disciplining the body and not succumbing to its craving to be pampered, indulged, and overly protected.

For when the body grows fat, the soul weakens. "We have such stingy hearts that it seems to us we're going to lose the earth if we desire to neglect the body a little for the sake of the spirit." Sometimes we need to push ourselves, test our limits, and neglect the body deliberately. It won't kill us to get up early, exercise more, and eat beans instead of meat or even fast altogether for a time. The virtue of discretion and a good dose of common sense tell us when to take care of the body and when to forget it for the sake of the spirit.

Celebration

TERESA WAS ALWAYS GRATEFUL for the gifts people sent her and considered them "marks of love": potatoes, butter, quince jam, orange-flower water, embroidery, cheese and lemons, dog-fish, shad, and seabream. (I love making these lists!) But tunny-fish? She left it in Malagón, "and long may it stay there!" She was enchanted when she saw her first coconuts: "Blessed be He who created them: they are certainly something worth seeing." She did not cut the new fruit open mechanically but ceremoniously, in a spirit of celebration.

Teresa teaches us how to celebrate even life's smallest events with joy and gratitude. When the coarse frieze clothing of her first band of sisters became infested with lice, she organized a procession with musical instruments and improvised a clever song, in the spirit of our modern-day "talking-blues":

You've clothed us now in livery new,
Heavenly King.
Should creatures vile infest our frieze,
Deliverance bring!
You who've come here prepared for death,
Yield not one whit,
And such vile creatures great or small,
Fear not at all.

The sisters gaily called the processional cross they carried "Christ of the lice" and the house was never infested again. (This very cross is preserved today in the museum of San José in Avila.) Teresa encouraged her followers to compose these couplets to celebrate any variety of occasions. She exchanged the verses with her sisters and sent them to Lorenzo:

We had a great festival yesterday: it was the Name of Jesus. God reward you (for your kindness). I don't know what I can send you in return for all the things you send me except these carols which I made up. My confessor had told me to amuse the sisters, so I spent several evenings with them, and I could think of no other way of entertaining them than this. They have a nice tune, if young Francisco could manage to sing it... I think these verses will touch you and arouse your devotion, only don't tell anyone I said so.

Only a small number of Teresa's poems have been preserved. They indicate that she was not a great poet but a woman with a gift for making every occasion special.

Several poems were written to celebrate Christmas. Teresa charmingly addresses shepherds she has named Giles, Llorente, Bras, and Menga. Since the Baby Jesus will come to a brutal death, Teresa urges Llorente to join her in stealing away the baby to protect him. She describes Mary, the Mother of God, as a shepherdess and amusingly asks, "Is she a relative of the Mayor?" Then she calls her the daughter of God, "glowing starlike." This description is much more beautiful in Spanish and accessible even to those who do not understand the language: *"Relumbra, como una estrella."*

Even Teresa's didactic poetry, usually written for women joining her communities, is interesting because of the imagery. Poem 31 was written antiphonally, Teresa on verses, her sisters on the chorus. Poem 28 calls the new nun a bride, betrothed to the King of Majesty, her heavenly spouse, whom Teresa calls husband and handsome shepherd in Poem 27. She loved to juxtapose marital imagery with martial imagery: marrying the king, serving the captain, fighting his battles. When we read Teresa's poems, we must remember that many were meant to be sung, accompanied by flute, tambourine, drum and castanets, for Teresa loved to sing and dance.

Teresa emphasized recreation as well as prayer, which was revolutionary in the religious communities of her day. "Anyone who works all the year round badly needs relaxation," she wrote to her Dominican friend Domingo Bañez, busy professor at the University of Salamanca. Teresa knew that life can be a heavy burden, so she encouraged recreation, leisure, and play to provide variation and relief. She did not permit formal games so that her nuns would be more creative in entertaining each other. This is a good lesson for us in a lazier era of television and computer games, social media and spectator sports.

"Here comes the Mother Foundress to share our recreation," sang little Isabel Dantisco as Teresa approached the common room. "So let us dance and let us sing and show our jubilation." But not all Teresa's sisters appreciated the lively atmosphere she created with poetry, music, and dance. "What, are we being asked to sing?" one of them once complained. "It would be better to contemplate." Teresa sent her to her room. "Don't take this amiss," she gently chided her. "We need everything that helps to make life bearable."

Humor

A GOOD SENSE OF HUMOR helps make life bearable. "God deliver us from sour-faced saints," Teresa quipped. She was a great laugher. Notice how often she writes, "I was amused" or "I laughed to myself." Her wry humor gives her writing wit, bite, satire, irony, and "edge." Her effective use of exclamation points helps us see the twinkle in her eye and catch her humorous tone!

How droll she found it when Antonio de Heredia began furnishing her first monastery for men not with beds or chairs but five clocks! Later in life, she teased him about not answering her letters. Did he take a vow not to write? She joked with one of his confrères about using inappropriate elegant forms of address and calling her "Madam." She laughed with Lorenzo because he sent her sweets, sardines and money, while all she gave him was hair-shirts! Then she teased him for being a "ladies' man," condoning it because the ladies were all nuns!

The more intimate the friend, the more Teresa teased. After a period of intense suffering, she wrote to Jerónimo Gracián: "I was amused to know that [you are] now wanting more trials again. Do, for the love of God, let us have a little respite, for they involve others beside yourself! Let us give them a few days' rest!" She also teased him about falling off his mule and about "those dreadful cod patties" he had to eat.

Teresa often found St. John of the Cross too serious. "God deliver me from people so spiritual that they want to turn everything into perfect contemplation, no matter what," she wrote him in jest. She called him "little Seneca" because he was so philosophical and "half a friar" because he was not even five feet tall!

But most of all, Teresa made fun of herself, teaching us not to take ourselves too seriously. "I can't remember any more. What a brain for a foundress!" she wrote to her brother. On the fortieth anniversary of taking the habit, she begged God to make her a "real nun of Carmel: better late than never!" Towards the end of her life she laughed because she had to travel to "a cold place in the cold weather and to the hottest place in the hottest time of the year. And then Father Nicolao would grumble about it! I really was amused at that!" Even as she lay dying in Alba de Tormes, she kept her gift of repartee. Asked whether she wanted to be buried back in Avila, she replied: "Can't they spare a handful of earth here?"

Teresa loved children and knew their innocent zest for life could brighten the dourest adult. She lived with both her niece Teresita, newly arrived from America, and Gracián's young sister Bella. She enjoyed Teresita "going about the house like a little fairy," entertaining everyone at recreation with tales about the Indians, becoming a better storyteller than Teresa herself, who was prized for her storytelling. Bella helped Teresa through some of her most trying times with her funny responses to reality. After Teresa gave her a piece of melon, she said: "Melon is so cold it deafens the throat." These episodes were an ongoing delight for Teresa as she spread her joy through letters to friends. And they continue to delight her readers today, five hundred years later.

Emotional Vitality

DELIGHT AND JOY, gratitude, wonder, laughter and celebration: life evokes all these feelings. Some of us experience too much feeling. We become over-emotional, hysterical, and irrational, which makes life difficult. But others find life even more difficult because of a low level of emotional awareness. We live blandly, protected by our defense mechanisms, emotionally flat, afraid to feel life in its total polarity. Wonder and delight escape us because we repress our anxiety. We do not experience enough laughter and joy because we block our sorrow and pain. We do not live in a spirit of celebration and gratitude because we run from suffering. Teresa teaches us a more integrated approach. She shows us how to take reality straight and undiluted, how to be at home with our feelings and express them openly.

In her letters, she admits to feeling frightened, irritated, shocked, cross, dreadfully grieved, full of immense distress and intolerable dislike. She writes: "I'm sick of talking about it," "I have been in the grip of depression," and "Really I am annoyed with Father Mariano for not forwarding the papers."

"How oppressed I have been feeling lately," she confides to Gracián. She's "nervous" because he's so far away, "troubled" because she can't get his advice, "disappointed" to think how often she writes and how few letters reach him. "I got angry," she confesses to Maria de San José. "I was treating you as one of my dearest daughters. It hurt me terribly not to find the same frankness and love in you." The possibility of Maria's illness made Teresa "unspeakably worried."

Throughout her major works, Teresa speaks frequently of her heart breaking into pieces. She knew how it felt to be totally incapacitated, weighed down and completely useless, "unable to think any good thing or want to do it." Like us, she sometimes felt numb, or terribly upset over trivial things that at other times would make her laugh. Her love of God became so lukewarm that she couldn't even remember the Holy One, who seemed so far away. Prayer and solitude meant nothing but more anguish. "Well then, what will this poor soul do when the torment goes on for many days?" she asked herself:

> *If it prays, it feels as though it hasn't prayed, as far as consolation goes, I mean. For consolation is not admitted into the soul's interior... solitude causes greater harm, and also another torment for this soul is that it be with anyone or that others speak to it. And thus however much it forces itself not to do so, it goes about with a gloomy and ill-tempered mien that is externally very noticeable.*

In a powerful lengthy passage from *The Way of Perfection* she admits how hard it is sometimes to live up to her ideals:

Sometimes I think I am very detached; and as a matter of fact when put to the test, I am. At another time I will find myself so attached, and perhaps to things that the day before I would have made fun of, that I almost don't know myself. At other times I think I have great courage and that I wouldn't turn from anything of service to God; and when put to the test, I do have this courage for some things. Another day will come in which I won't find the courage in me to kill even an ant for God if in doing so I'd meet with any opposition. In like manner it seems to me that I don't care at all about things or gossip said of me; and when I'm put to the test this is at times true—indeed I am pleased about what they say. Then there come days in which one word alone distresses me, and I would want to leave the world because it seems everything is a bother to me.

Teresa often got so angry she wanted to "eat everyone up, without being able to help it; or it would seem to me an accomplishment if one could control one's temper." In two of her most poignant images, she describes herself as a helpless bird with broken wings or a stupid little donkey grazing. Teresa was no stranger to fear. "I was frightened and scared," she confessed. "With the serious heart trouble that I had, I'm amazed that much damage wasn't done to me." She worried about going insane because no one understood her and considered this one of the most severe trials in her life.

True and False Tears

LIVING A VIBRANT EMOTIONAL LIFE often leads to tears. When is it appropriate to cry and when not? Teresa offers some healthy advice. She spent a lot of her life weeping. It is fascinating to trace her attitude toward tears from her more hysterical early years to the calmer wisdom of her mature years.

As a teenager, Teresa felt she suffered from hardness of heart: she could read the entire Gospel account of the Passion of Jesus without shedding a tear. This pained her terribly, and she envied anyone who could cry. By her early twenties, Teresa was weeping profusely.

She distinguishes between two kinds of tears: those we induce through our own effort, and the "gift of tears" God gives, which we are unable to resist. Teresa experienced both. At first she highly valued her weeping, but then she began to criticize herself for "fraudulent tears" she thought were "womanish and without strength." (I doubt she would use the word "womanish" today.)

By the time she turned sixty-two and completed *The Interior Castle,* Teresa was highly critical of "false tears" and the harm they do. "Arduous tears" leave us so exhausted, we're left unfit for prayer. "Anxious tears" are brought on by our uncontrolled passions, and we are no better as a result of them. Our sobbing gives us headaches, tight chests and nosebleeds, leaving us too weak to pray. We may think we are weeping for God, but we are not: we are really feeling sorry for ourselves and inducing the tears. When God gives the genuine gift of tears, they comfort us and bring peace, not turbulence. In the end, she said, we should always be suspicious of tears, forget about weeping and "set our hands to the task of hard work and virtue."

Hard work and virtue are not as zesty as comets and thunderclaps, water and fire, lightning and laughter, celebration and even lice. But for Teresa, the hard work of virtue was every bit as exciting: the beauty of humility that enables us to see the grandeur of God beyond our own inflated egos, the wonder of poverty that helps us perceive the richness beyond material possessions, and the nobility of courage, which makes us undertake heroic quests for God and the planet.

Earth, Exile and Eternity

WE NEED TO DISTINGUISH between the earth, which Teresa clearly considered good, and the world, which she sharply criticized. By "world" she meant that network of elements that conspire against God and God's work in us, summed up in vanity, selfishness, self-love, and egotism. Though we walk lovingly upon the earth God created and called good, we must "wage war" against the world and "trample it underfoot." When Teresa uses "earthly" as a negative adjective, she usually means "worldly."

"How quickly all things come to an end," she sighed, painfully aware of the perishability of life. Flowers in the field fade away, coconuts and cold melons disappear as soon as they're eaten, celebrations and rhyming verses are soon forgotten.

Teresa's most frequent metaphor for the pain of impermanence is "exile." She contrasts, but does not separate, the exile of our earthly life with eternal life in our true home beyond death. In her poem "Sighs in Exile," Teresa feels tormented, like a fish caught on a painful hook. She intersperses her cries of agony with loving names for God. Later in her *Foundations*, she thanks God for the power of only one of these many sighs.

She urges us not to overrate the earth and turn it into an idol, but to see it instead as a metaphor for the eternal. This earthly exile is characterized by inevitable insecurity, instability, and change, which must be graciously integrated. How did Teresa cope? She prayed:

Oh, God help me, what a miserable life this is! There's no secure happiness, nor anything that doesn't change. A short time before it seemed to me I wouldn't change my happiness with anyone on earth, and now the very reason for this happiness tormented me in such a way that I didn't know what to do with myself. Oh, if we would carefully observe the affairs of our life! Each one would see through experience the little of either happiness or unhappiness he ought to have on their account.

In our exile we are trapped in what Teresa calls the "valley of grieving" where all we get is "sips." And Teresa, in her zest for life, with her longing for God and divine fullness, wanted big gulps! Even as a child, she was fascinated by "forever." Her little girl mind already had some primitive intuition of eternity in the face of earthly ephemerality. Her insights may help us ignore the trivia in our lives and center our attention on what lasts forever.

"All things pass, God never changes." These lines from Teresa's famous "bookmark prayer" recur throughout her writings and lead her to ecstatic meditations on death: "O death, death, I don't know who fears you, since life lies in you!" We are only pilgrims on this earth, en route to our true country. There is another world beyond this life, she believes. Death will not be like going to a foreign country but like finally going home.

CONVERSATION TWO
Agony and Ecstasy

TERESA'S PRAYER was as colorful and flamboyant as her life. The wild woman of Avila used vibrant, sensuous, and earthy imagery to describe prayer. She considered these descriptions coarse, rough, and inelegant. "I am laughing to myself because they do not satisfy me. But I don't know any others." Teresa tended to be too hard on herself. I find her metaphors for both the agony and ecstasy of prayer dynamic and engaging.

In the agony of prayer, we may feel like exiles in a foreign country, caught in the teeth of a terrifying dragon, or struck by lightning and reduced to ashes. Sometimes we feel on fire with thirst but unable to get to the water. We feel as though we are drowning in flood tides and cannot get out of the river. We may feel bitten by odious reptiles. We may want to fly but find ourselves bound in chains. Sometimes we seem to fight with a giant, lose all our energy, and end up exhausted. The agony of prayer may be so intense, it feels as though a suffocating rope is around our necks.

Prayer was not always easy for Teresa, any more than it is for us. At times the very thought of prayer saddened and depressed her. "For some years," she admits in her *Life,* "I was more anxious that the hour I had determined to spend in prayer be over than I was to remain there, and more anxious to listen for the striking of the clock." How encouraging for those of us who are just beginning! Even the great St. Teresa had to force herself to pray: "So unbearable was the sadness I felt on entering the chapel that I had to muster up all my courage."

When prayer is this difficult, we need determination to persevere. "I had to use courage against myself," Teresa wrote, advising us to use similar courage. When prayer becomes a burden, we must go to extremes and apply stringent discipline. When we remain faithful to prayer, it becomes easier, and we no longer have to work so hard. Prayer ceases to be an effort and becomes a delight. But "this cannot be learned without a little trouble," Teresa cautions us. If we are to experience prayer as ecstasy, we must first experience it as agony and take the trouble to pray.

Getting to prayer and staying there, despite a hundred good reasons for being somewhere else and doing something else that seems at the moment infinitely more worthwhile, very often requires a fierce determination of will. But Teresa herself says, "After I had made this effort, I found myself with greater delight than sometimes when I had the desire to pray." Troublesome prayer can very often be the most rewarding. We should not hesitate to pray, even when we don't feel like it.

Teresa tells us over and over again that we need a great deal of resolute determination to persevere until reaching the end. Come what may, whatever work is involved, whatever criticism arises, whether we arrive or whether we die in the process, even if we don't have courage for the trials that come our way, even if the world collapses around us, we've got to keep going. In the Sixth Mansion of her *Interior Castle,* Teresa gives us a long list of trials we can expect if we want to be men and woman of prayer. She suffered all these herself and speaks powerfully out of her personal experience. She did not let any of these agonies hold her back. Neither should we.

"Pay Now!"

IN HER WARM AND WOMANLY WAY, Teresa encourages us to persevere. We often see this in the saints and sages we meet today. When we talk about our own trials and difficulties, they say with similar warmth and compassion: "It's all worth it. I wouldn't trade it for the world." Teresa says the same: "The time will come when you will understand how trifling everything else is next to so precious a reward."

When I read the spiritual classics, I pay careful attention to the punctuation. Whenever the author uses exclamation points, I know great drama, emotion, or a wry sense of humor is being expressed. Teresa uses many exclamation points. Her writings are also full of "Ohs," as she speaks spontaneously from her impassioned soul. Thank goodness no editors have soberly deleted these, because they give us a true sense of how Teresa was feeling as she wrote. "Oh, God help me," she said, as she described the painful effort and the glorious rewards of prayer: "How you afflict your lovers! But everything is small in comparison with what you give them afterward."

We tend to be easily discouraged, so it helps to look at multiple "reward" passages from Teresa and imbibe more of her contagious enthusiasm. "All the trials endured for the sake of enjoying God are well worthwhile. Before we die, He will pay for everything at once." Teresa's terminology is amusing here, as she talks about God "paying off." In one of the passages I cite most often counseling those in beginning stages of prayer, Teresa writes: "He does not keep the reward of loving Him for the next life alone. The pay begins in this life." She continues: "Were we to serve the Lord through severe trials for a great number of years, we would feel well repaid for it." Before we have much personal experience of this, we may be cynical and doubtful. But if we persevere, we conclude with Teresa: "I would not exchange these trials for all the world's treasures."

The Ecstasy of Prayer

WE NEED COURAGE FOR THE PRAYER of agony precisely because we need even more courage for the prayer of ecstasy. How can this be? Teresa clearly explains that the prayer of ecstasy is often more incredible, more exhausting, and more unbearable in its wonder.

Here is a passage from the Sixth Mansion, where she writes not about trials and tribulations, but ecstasy and rapture: "You will laugh at my saying this and think I'm foolish. It will seem to you that such courage is unnecessary and there's no woman so miserable who wouldn't have the courage to be married to the King." (Teresa frequently refers to God as His Majesty, the King.) Then she concludes emphatically: "I tell you there is need for more courage than you think." She is certain that if

God were not to give us courage, no matter how good we might find the favor or the ecstasy, it would be impossible to experience the rapture if God did not strengthen us to bear it.

Teresa's metaphors for the ecstasy of prayer are once again colorful, dramatic, and flamboyant. This prayer is like being raised up by a mighty eagle and carried aloft on its wings, drowning in an infinite sea of supreme truth or quickly reaching the end of a long journey and finding everything all at once. Prayer is like being in a garden where the fragrance of the flowers permeates the entire atmosphere (Teresa had a particularly sensitive sense of smell), or being inebriated with divine wine. In a uniquely Spanish image, Teresa says prayer is like watching a bullfight. If we pray, we're like the people in the stands, safe from the bull. If we don't pray, we're defenselessly down in the arena, confronted by a raging, snorting animal.

Ecstatic prayer is a shining sun and a tremendous Yes! In earthly matters there is both "yes" and "no," but in this prayer there is only "yes." "No" only comes afterward, when our delight ends and we cannot recover it. In this prayer, we may feel like a tiny bird, tired of flying, in great need of rest. God suddenly comes and picks us up, laying us gently in the nest. Using more biblical expressions, the prayer of ecstasy is like being the thirsty deer who finally gets to the water, the dove who finally finds the olive branch, or the bride who finally receives the bridegroom's kiss.

All these descriptions are graphic, physical, and earthy. How could we expect anything but an earthy approach from a woman who once loved perfume and wore bright orange?

Teresa knew that prayer is earthy because God, too, is earthy. "Lord, You are on the earth and clothed with it," she marveled. Everything on earth, then, becomes the stuff of our prayer. Prayer does not erupt only in designated religious places, in the presence of specially designated objects, persons, or rituals, or at specifically scheduled times. Real prayer erupts everywhere and any time. We must not become prayer-conscious but God-conscious, and bring all of life into our prayer. We must be earthy mystics: not only mystical—too misty; and not merely earthy—too vulgar. Tension between the two creates a more dynamic and balanced spirituality.

Holy Sensuousness

PRAYER IN THE TERESIAN SPIRIT includes all five senses: smell, sight, sound, touch, and taste. Teresa sometimes felt a powerful fragrance spreading through all her senses, as though a sweet ointment were poured into the marrow of her bones. Sometimes it felt as if a flaming brazier in her innermost depths was exuding a sweet-smelling perfume.

How amusing that Teresa was every bit as affected by unpleasant odors as she was by pleasing fragrances! When she erred, she thought she smelled bad. In her *Way of Perfection,* she urges us to thank God for generously tolerating the terrible odor of our "sinfulness." It's amusing enough that Teresa calls herself a worm when she feels bad; but to make matters worse, she calls herself a "foul-smelling" worm! When life was good, everything smelled wonderful. But when life went wrong, Teresa smelled a foul stench.

We need a good sense of taste in our life of prayer. Teresa frequently describes the experience of prayer in terms of food and drink. God is so in love with us, we sit at the Divine's own table, sharing divine food, even taking a portion from God's own mouth. How sweet this fruit is! Teresa raves about the different kinds of food we take from God: the taste will be according to our preference "already cut, cooked, and even chewed." Initially we are sustained by milk from the divine breasts. Then we are nourished with apples. And finally, the King brings us into his wine cellar.

No two lives of prayer are ever the same. Our prayer will not be the same as Teresa's. But to grow in a healthy life of prayer under Teresa's earthy influence, we must come to our senses! We must live sensuously: see as much as we can see, touch as much as we can touch, taste as much as we can taste.

Some people falsely presume that sensuousness is antithetical to prayer. In imbalanced eras and areas of Christian spirituality, we are taught to ignore and even annihilate our senses. This error is not part of the solid Christian mystical tradition or the teaching of Jesus. In the spirit of the Gospel, the Christian mystical tradition is sensuous indeed. We make a terrible mistake in both our humanity and our prayer when we try to kill our senses, thereby destroying an entire realm of prayer. St. Ignatius of Loyola, the Basque soldier who founded the Jesuits during the early years of Teresa's century, devised a method of meditation which incorporated all five senses. But this teaching was feared and forgotten only fifty years after the death of Ignatius in 1556. We must not repudiate but refine our senses, by more discriminating use.

Although one school of Christian thought believes in a separation between physical and spiritual senses, it may be more appropriate to speak of transformation rather than replacement. There is no discontinuity between our physical and spiritual senses. If our physical senses atrophy through disuse or grow dull through riotous overuse, we lose our spiritual sensitivity. Spiritual sensitivity heightens when we know how to see, touch, and taste the physical world with exquisite reverence and contemplative discipline. This often means not more sensation on the horizontal plane in a greedy multiplication of experiences, but deeper vertical experience of singular reality: one white peony, one glass of wine, one luscious kiss, one rousing volleyball game, one beloved constellation in the sky. Teresa urges us to cultivate our physical senses for the sake of a more integrated inner life.

Vision of God

THE SENSE OF SIGHT may be the most important in prayer, as it usually is in the whole of life. Teresa explains how prayer is looking at the One who is looking at us. When we heighten our awareness, we understand that God never takes loving eyes off us. What is wrong with us that we do not keep our eyes on the Divine?

I've often read the lives of saints and mystics and wanted to ask: "But exactly what did you do in your prayer?" Teresa tells us. Her answer is similar to St. Francis, who said: "I look at God, and God looks at me." This is what Christian mystics mean when they use technical terms such as the "prayer of simple regard." These categories can be confusing and misleading. But graphic descriptions from Francis and Teresa ground us in life experience. Prayer is looking at God who is looking at us.

Teresa teaches it is important "not to think much but to love much." Though thinking and reasoning play a crucial role at certain stages, when we move into the more contemplative aspects of prayer, excessive rationality spoils and even precludes prayer. Teresa's entire teaching on mystical prayer can be summed up in one simple phrase: "Just look at him."

As Roman Catholics, we look at God made palpably present in the Holy Sacrifice of the Mass, continuing the sacred presence in the tabernacle. Jesus is as tangibly present to us today, in what we call the Blessed Sacrament, as he was when he walked the earth. We're tempted to say, "Oh, if only I could have looked on Jesus then, it would be easy for me." But if we do not sense the sacramental presence of God now, what makes us think we would have responded to God's physical presence then?

So look at God on the altar or in the Blessed Sacrament. Look at the Divine in the world of nature, revealed in earth and air, fire and water, flower and tree. Look at God in the sacred scriptures, weeping over Jerusalem, laughing with the children, teasing with those wonderful women we meet in the Gospels. Look at the Holy One in the faces of your children, your spouses, in the faces of your neighbors, in your gardens and your animals.

I have seen God dramatically enfleshed in my animals: Zorba, the old English sheepdog with the soulful shepherding eyes; Tate, the noble cat who lived with me for twenty years, no matter where I moved; Rags, the wild cottontail rabbit who ate out of my hand after a winter in my woodpile. I've seen God in the innocence and powerlessness of my brother with Down Syndrome, who died of leukemia at age eight; in the agony of my mother, crucified to her dialysis machine; in the zest of my ribald father eating watermelon, clams, or corn on the cob.

"I'm not asking you to do anything more than look at Him," begs St. Teresa. "He's not waiting for anything else but that you look at Him."

Holy Madness, Martha and Mary

TERESA USUALLY WRITES CLEARLY and lucidly. But when she describes prayer as holy madness, she becomes endearingly mad herself as she exclaims: "I don't know any other terms for describing it besides madness, foolishness, and this delightful disquiet. The soul doesn't know what to do. It doesn't know whether it should be quiet or whether it should speak out. It doesn't know whether it should laugh or whether it should weep." Then Teresa begins to pray: "O help me, God. Sometimes I find it a remedy to speak folly in a thousand ways, or to speak in absurdities. My King, I beseech you, make everyone I speak to mad with your love, or don't make me speak to them at all." Wanting all of us to enjoy this blessed madness, she continues: "May we all be sick with this kind of sickness. May we all be mad for love of Him who for love of us was called mad!"

One of Teresa's countrymen was Miguel de Unamuno, who died of a broken heart in 1936 after the Spanish Civil War. Unamuno, who wrote *The Tragic Sense of Life* and always dressed in black, also wrote a commentary on the Spanish classic, *Don Quixote,* in which he insisted that the aging knight of La Mancha went mad on purpose, "out of well-seasoned maturity." Had she known Quixote, Teresa may well have agreed. So the next broad Teresian recommendation we learn for growing in the spiritual life is precisely this: Go mad!

We may well say: "This is madness," thinking that wild Teresian prayer is fine for some, but not for us. After all, we're sensible: we have jobs, families, important ministries, global concerns. Is it possible that we use our noble responsibilities to evade our primary responsibility to be men and women of God, men and women of prayer?

Teresa is a great model precisely because she was so busy. She is not only one of the greatest contemplatives in the Western spiritual tradition, but also one of its greatest activists. Tremendously involved with people and projects, constantly on the go, Teresa still found time to make prayer a priority.

She founded new convents at the rate of one and sometimes two per year. She travelled all over Spain on abominable roads, in frightful weather, staying in dirty terrible inns. (No wonder she often referred to this painful earthly existence as a "'night in a bad inn.") She dealt with businessmen, irate civil and ecclesiastical authorities, hostile towns, ignorant advisors and superiors, petty and jealous women within her own ranks. She was an ingenious administrator with a flair for organization, an astute diplomat, and wise in the world of finance, litigation, and contract negotiation. Her financial worries, business deals, and personnel problems certainly challenged her life of prayer, but never spoiled it.

As she grappled with this tension in her busy life, Teresa frequently meditated on the story of Martha and Mary in the Gospel of Luke. Remember how Jesus loved these sisters and their brother, Lazarus, and often stayed with them as he hiked the long roads from Galilee to Jerusalem. Mary sat enraptured at the feet of Jesus, gazing into his face and absorbing every word that fell from his beloved lips. Martha busied herself in the kitchen and resented Mary's "idleness." Jesus sympathized with Martha, but explained that Mary had chosen "the better part."

We may try to escape the demands of prayer by setting up a false dichotomy between Martha and Mary, making "either-or" what Jesus intended to be "both-and." The Marthas say work is the primary spiritual mode; the Marys say prayer is. Some may say they are more Martha than Mary to justify compulsive action and addiction to work. Others may say they are more Marian to justify inertia. Neither one of these extremes is valid.

Teresa resolves the conflict well in her own life and teachings, though not easily. She makes it clear that Martha and Mary belong together. It's possible to be both Martha and Mary simultaneously. In every one of her major writings, Teresa refers to this crucial balance: Martha and Mary are sisters. Martha and Mary live together. Martha and Mary are one. We need to rejoice in Martha's action and in Mary's contemplation as well.

As we grow in the life of prayer, we paradoxically become more Martha than Mary. When a young novice begged Teresa to teach her the art of prayer, she expected to be given additional "free time" and sent to the chapel. Instead Teresa sent her to the kitchen and said: "Learn to pray among the pots and pans."

Stealing Time

WHEN OUR LIFE IS CROWDED and busy and we have no time for solitude, we think we have the perfect excuse for not praying. Teresa tells us this is no excuse at all. Deep in our hearts, we know she's right. Prayer is primarily an expression of love. It isn't helpful to believe that without solitude, there is no time for prayer. Even in the midst of business matters, God is still a companion.

Teresa herself had very little time, especially in the last twenty-five years of her life. She frequently lamented: "I don't have any time. I have no calm. I'm worried about a thousand different things. I've got a terrible headache. I'm writing this in a hurry." She always lived in poor houses where she had to share an enormous amount of manual labor. In later years, Teresa was overwhelmed by the details of administration. Then where did she find time for prayer? How did she manage to grow to such mystical heights?

She tells us almost sheepishly: "I stole the time. When I didn't have the time, I stole it." This is another great secret from the lives of men and women of real prayer. Like Teresa, they are not the ones who have the time to pray. They are the ones who take the time. This is a tremendous comfort to me personally. When I joined the Spiritual Life Institute in 1967, I thought I was going to be given vast spaces of time for prayer. Instead, I was crushed almost immediately with the burdens of leadership. I had to learn, and learn the hard way, that if I was to become a woman of prayer, I would have to make the time. But how?

There are three practical ways to find this precious time. They have worked well not only for me, but for hundreds of others I've met, struggling to learn the secret to living more contemplatively in the midst of busy active lives. The first is to steal time, the way Teresa did. The second is to reclaim lost time or stop wasting time. The third is to celebrate the timelessness God gives us every Sabbath.

How do we steal time? We steal it from ourselves and from our sleep. We can get up earlier in the morning before everyone else, a perfect time to pray. Or stay up later at night, when everyone else has gone to bed. It helps sometimes to get up in the middle of the night for no other reason than to pray. Set the alarm, get up and pray, then go back to bed. The body needs to adjust to these changes and tires easily at first. But we needn't stop on the first, second, or third day simply because of fatigue. If we continue to stretch our limits, we will adapt.

Prayer can be more refreshing than sleep. I learned this years ago when I was challenged to sleep less and find other ways to be recreated. The Gospels tell us over and over again: "Stay awake." Teresa regularly returns to this theme: if we want to enjoy intimacy with God, we must not go to sleep.

Reclaiming Lost Time

WE CAN LEARN TO STOP wasting time and recover the time we waste. I found it so revealing when I wanted to find more time for prayer and began to hold myself more accountable. "There are twenty-four hours in the day," I said to myself. "Exactly what do I do with them?" I watched myself very carefully, kept "time logs," and was astonished at how much time I spent on inconsequential matters.

This is a fruitful exercise. Look at the days of your own life. Record how much time you spend doing this and that. Notice how much time you may fritter away, "hanging out," doing nothing in particular, nothing fruitful or contemplative, perhaps talking on the phone, daydreaming, flipping through magazines or glancing at the newspaper, reading mediocre literature. We could be in the depths of prayer, enjoying spousal intimacy with God, being uplifted and refreshed, and yet we often prefer to "hang out."

Teresa's life leads us to an amazing reflection: it was not work that kept Teresa from prayer. She wasted too much time in the convent parlor, engaged in frivolous conversation that had no deep or enduring value. It didn't inspire or refresh her. It brought no joy or enlightenment. It wasn't even genuine enlivening hilarity. It was simply meaningless chit-chat that dissipated her energy and robbed her of time, a spirit of recollection and self-possession. The computer desk or TV room may be the modern equivalent of Teresa's parlor. We've all read surveys which show that the average person in the U.S. watches far too much television and spends too much time at the computer. How many hours do we spend sitting in front of a screen, instead of being more creative and contemplative?

The third way to find time for prayer is to celebrate the Sabbath. God created the Seventh Day to give us rest from deadlines, pressures and clock time. The Sabbath is a timeless day we can spend in the spaciousness of "eternity." Celebrating Sabbath is a radical counter-cultural effort to overcome a crucial Western malaise, which author and drama critic Walter Kerr called the "neurotic compulsion to work." The Sabbath is not a day to balance the checkbook, wash the car, or mow the lawn. Sabbath is a day for the highest human acts: playing and praying.

CONVERSATION THREE
Spousal Prayer

CONTEMPLATION AND MYSTICISM are synonymous terms. They both mean *loving experiential awareness of God:* not ideas in the head or on the lips, but personal living experience. In the Teresian tradition, this experience takes a special form which spiritual writer William McNamara calls "spousal prayer." As he wrote in *The Human Adventure,* in spousal prayer we come to know God the way a human spouse knows the spouse, the way a friend knows a friend, the way a lover knows the beloved. Spousal prayer is for men and women, for married couples and celibates, for people raising children or living in monasteries.

If married people relegate spousal prayer to celibate life, they may miss a whole realm of prayer that could be theirs. This experience is not only for the celibate who does not have a human spouse. Even if we have a husband or wife, God longs to be our Divine Spouse.

Both men and women ask how spousal prayer affects their marital relationships. This depends on the marriage. Those who enjoy healthy marriages, full of spousal soul-sharing as well as sexual vitality, find their marriages enhanced. Those in unhealthy marriages often find it easier to relate to their spouses because of the divine intimacy they experience.

Both men and women in unhappy marriages sometimes turn to spirituality to compensate for their lack of intimacy on the human level. This is not necessarily unhealthy, but it can lead to unhealthy pietistic mood-altering and addiction to religion. Sometimes an angry husband blurts out, "I'm losing my wife." I say, "You already lost her long ago. What are you going to do now to woo her back? And how will you continue to cherish her?"

Spousal prayer does not make God the divine rival of a human spouse. Human love prefigures divine love. Spiritual matrimony with God may be the goal of our human longings. Is this our real desire when we marry another human person? In the deepest relationships, lovers do not turn each other into idols, but recognize one another as icons, leading them through their love into the very bosom of the Godhead. How fortunate those who find the Divine Lover embodied in the human one! How unlucky those who don't! For ultimately there may only be one love-affair, and that is our love-affair with God.

Consecrated celibates make formal religious vows and promise poverty, chastity, and obedience. But there is really only one vow, the wedding vow. When we consecrate ourselves to religious life, as I have, we take God as our spouse. This mystical dimension of the vowed life, sometimes obscured in our day, needs to be rediscovered. Women religious used to wear wedding rings and considered the veil a bridal veil. In the wake of Vatican II, many of these women removed their rings and took off their habits. When people I first meet see the ring I wear on my left hand, they are initially perplexed, then surprised when I say, "I am a bride of Christ." The idea is new to many, and they are pleased. When they hear Leonard Cohen sing "Joan of Arc," they find deeper meaning in the image of the virginal Joan's wedding dress hung in ashes above the fiery stake of her martyrdom.

Men may be less attracted to spousal prayer, but they are also called to it. I am a woman, and Christ the Bridegroom incarnated in Jesus was masculine, so my viewpoint is obviously feminine. But this by no means eliminates any man. Every man has a feminine dimension, and every woman a masculine one. Both masculine and feminine principles must be wed in us if we are to become truly whole. The teachings of Swiss psychologist Carl Jung on the *animus* and *anima* may help us understand.

The essential point is simple: Men can no longer be "all-male." This leads to imbalanced behavior that devalues and exploits women, destroys the earth in greedy domination and over-consumption, and robs men of human qualities as manly as they are feminine: vulnerability and surrender, tenderness and nurturing. Nor can women continue to be "all-female." This leads to imbalanced behavior that devalues men by manipulating them, evades responsibility for determining the future of society, and robs women of human qualities as womanly as they are masculine: strength and courage, initiative and the "warrior spirit."

In relation to the "Hound of Heaven," haunting, pursuing, and wooing us, we are all feminine. In many languages around the world, the word for "soul" is feminine: *psyche* in Greek, *anima* in Latin, *alma* in Spanish. How can this be true for a man? John of the Cross, one of the greatest Western mystics, gives an answer in *The Spiritual Canticle*, his meditation on The Song of Songs. According to one translator of this magnificent poetry: "You make my soul feel like a woman." This does not mean that John of the Cross sacrificed his masculinity. Some of the greatest bridal mystics have been strong men such as St. Augustine and St. Bernard of Clairvaux.

Erotic Energy

I THINK SPOUSAL PRAYER is for everyone, at least part of the time. In the Christian spiritual tradition, we usually respond to God as Father, Brother, Lord, Master, Friend, and sometimes as Mother. But there are times when it is more appropriate to relate to God as Spouse. For some people this dimension predominates, especially those steeped in Carmelite spirituality. Prayer is personal and unique to each individual, and we must respect and encourage variations. But if we never consider the possibility of spousal prayer, we cut ourselves off from new realms of divine intimacy.

Some people are repelled by the idea of spousal prayer and dismiss it as anthropomorphic, an aberration concocted by neurotic celibates to compensate for the absence of genital sexuality in their lives. But spousal prayer is "normal" and a revered dimension of the Christian mystical tradition. As British philosopher E.I. Watkin wrote decades ago, mysticism is not disguised sex; sex is disguised mysticism.

All of us possess a fundamental human quality described in a number of ways: eros, passion, libido, sexual, affective, or erotic energy. No matter what words we use, we understand the reality: a powerful energy almost synonymous with the life-force within us. A good definition comes from William McNamara's *Mystical Passion*. The author presents passion as "the breakthrough virtue," vital to spiritual development. He calls eros a reaching and stretching of the whole body-person for the fullness of life.

He also distinguishes between eros and eroticism. Eros, great-souled desire for oneness, is the beginning of mysticism. Eroticism, which he understands as preoccupation with genitality, is a deflection of real erotic energy and may limit our mystical possibilities.

We live in an over-genital and under-erotic culture. True eros means more than being "good in bed," although it can include that. The genital celebration of eros is only one viable alternative. If we stop here, we may stunt our growth, for true eros relates us profoundly to the entire universe. Let me quote McNamara at length here, where he draws heavily on the work of psychologist, Rollo May:

> *Eros, which is the Greek word for passion, is not synonymous with sexual titillation or what we commonly refer to as "eroticism." The Greeks emphasized eros; that is why that Greek word is so familiar to us. They deemphasized sex; that is why we hardly know what term they used for it. Eros pertains essentially to the art of making love* (coming into union—*communion). Sex is limited to the manipulation of organs. Eros attracts and lures us into union with everything. Eros is wakeful, vigilant, remembering whatever is true and beautiful, whatever is good. Sex is a need; eros is a desire. The sex act*

is, indeed, the most potent symbolic and specific celebration of relatedness imaginable. But eros is relatedness. Excitement accompanies sex. Tenderness dominates the erotic quest.

Eros is the longing to enjoy such deep and wide-ranged dimensions of relatedness—all originating from a critical center and tending toward an ultimate end—that a unitive and beautifying fruition of Being is experienced, at least incipiently and intermittently, on this earth. Although dramatically and supremely important in a good sexual relationship, the same erotic desire for union plays a central part in our rapport with animal and plant life, as well as with aesthetic, philosophical, ethical, scientific, socio-political, and religious forms. Eros relates us not only to other persons whom we love, but to the pig we are raising, the house we are building, the car we are driving, the vocation we are following. If we had been sufficiently charged with eros, for instance, we would have participated in a reverent dialogue with our environment which would have precluded the ecological disaster we are now suffering.

We all feel eros. Most people use it genitally. Our often sex-crazed society seems to believe that the only way to be happy and healthy is to utilize erotic energy genitally, as if we were pressure cookers about to burst. This attitude is primitive, psychologically debilitating, and spiritually destructive, as we learn from our growing awareness of sexual addiction, date-rape, and even rape within marriage. To help offset the erotomania that cripples our culture, we need strong integrated celibate men and women and faithful, chaste, married lovers committed to spousal prayer.

Throughout history, men and women around the world have expended their erotic energy in a variety of creative alternatives: great works of art and music, heroic exploration of wild frontiers, scientific research, profound scholarship, poetry, and literature. Some people channel this raw undifferentiated energy into the service of their country or some noble cause for the sake of the planet. And many have poured it into their love of God, their prayer, their mystical life. We call this transformation of erotic energy "sublimation."

Sublimation

I used to hate the word sublimation. I mistakenly thought it meant rejection or repression. It does not. When we sublimate, we transform erotic energy and make it sublime. (This does not mean that erotic energy expressed genitally cannot be sublime!) We redirect and channel it into another direction as a healthy and freely chosen alternative to genitality. Recapturing this fundamental understanding of sublimation, we restore its nobility and grandeur.

I was enormously helped years ago by a French priest-psychiatrist, Ignace Lepp. Three years before his death in 1966, Lepp published a study entitled *The Psychology of Loving*. (Parts of the book are now outdated.) In his final chapter, "The Sublimation of Love," he states: "From the psychological point of view, it is undeniable that the affective energy which the mystic consumes in the love of

God is the same as that which others make use of in erotic love, friendship, scientific or artistic dedication."

He then goes on to explain that sublimation is not a deviation but a sign of psychological health and integration. This conclusion helps us understand how many people throughout history and in our own day opt for celibacy, and not for religious or even spiritual reasons. Celibacy seems tacitly approved if your occupation is more secular. If you're a scholar or an astronomer and celibate because of your dedication to the stars or your study, society doesn't label you negatively as it may the Catholic priest or nun. Those who are critical of celibacy in the religious life need to be aware of its value and prevalence in other fields. Sublimation and spousal prayer are normal, human and healthy.

Mysticism or Neurosis

PREPARATION FOR CELIBACY is not always adequate. If we do not recognize the existence of erotic energy, and its power to transform or destroy us, our simple desire to live chastely may not be sufficient. We see this all too clearly today in the scandals involving not only Christian clergy but teachers from every spiritual tradition.

The celibate seems to have only two choices: mysticism or neurosis. If we are celibate but not mystical, we may end up neurotic. I know celibates whose neuroses are basically sexual, who have not come to terms with their fundamental erotic energy and do not channel it creatively. Surprised by the strength of their erotic impulses, they repress them and then become compulsive about food, alcohol, work, golf, talk, or even antiseptic tidiness.

It isn't easy to sublimate our sexual energy and be faithful to chastity in celibate or married life. We need to be more open and share our honest difficulties with one another in appropriate ways. Many great saints were not altogether free from neurotic deviations in their own struggles with channeling erotic energy. St. Anthony the Hermit kept seeing naked ladies under the bushes. St. Augustine prayed: "Oh God, give me chastity, but not yet." The celebrated St. Francis once made a family out of snow, a father, mother, and child. When asked what he was doing, he replied: "I may father a child yet."

Some people, startled by the frankness of St. Teresa's erotic energy, consider her neurotic. Others present her as a paragon of normalcy. Because of her passionate temperament and her penchant for falling in love, channeling eros was not always easy. Teresa does not speak the language of contemporary psychology and never explicitly mentions eros, libido, or sexual energy. But she was certainly aware of them and grappling with them in her own life and the lives of her followers, who were both men and women. She struggled for years with emotional addiction to men, which she refers to as "attachment." I treat this more extensively in the chapter entitled "Man-Woman" in my book on St. Teresa's mystical writings.

The Song of Songs

THE INTIMATE EXPERIENCE of God will differ from person to person. But the best description compares this prayer to spousal union between man and woman. As Teresa explains in the Fifth Mansion of her *Interior Castle,* there is no better comparison. When we consider spousal prayer, we use the language of human love.

Both human love and the spousal love of God meet magnificently in The Song of Songs, also called The Canticle of Canticles or The Song of Solomon, one of the most mysterious treasures of the Judeo-Christian tradition. What is this book doing in the Bible? Some call it a song of "profane love" and insist that it made its way into Holy Scripture by mistake and never should have been included. Others strongly believe that the love described in such sensuous terms has nothing to do with physical human love but is a perfect metaphor for mystical love between God and the soul. The greatest saints and lovers recognize both.

When we view The Song of Songs as poetry, out of the context of any religious tradition, we glean fresh insight. A ragged paperback called *A Treasury of Great Poems,* from our old library in Nova Scotia, presents the entire Song with this charming introduction: "There it is, a divine irrelevance, a passionately living, frankly sexual love poem in the midst of Holy Writ. The surcharged images and burning apostrophes follow the grim cynicisms of Ecclesiastes and precede the rapt prophecies of Isaiah. Never has there been a more magnificently inappropriate setting for a collection of amorous lyric poems."

The editor, Louis Untermeyer, asks in a spirit of wonder: "What are we to make of this?" He continues: "We may doubt that the Bible as a whole is a word-for-word inspiration, but who can doubt that these songs were inspired? They are unquestionably the word of God." Then with poetic humor and exuberance, badly needed in scripture scholars, he concludes: "The tireless Creator, the cosmic Author, was never happier, never more delightfully naive and lyrically exalted, never more in love with life than when he dictated The Song of Songs."

Both Jews and Christians have made The Song of Songs a canonical book of the Bible. This conveys the true and earthy spirit of these long traditions. Many of the greatest Christian mystics have written commentaries, from Origen in the third century, Jerome, Augustine, Bede the Venerable, Gregory of Nyssa, and on to the extensive work of Bernard of Clairvaux in the twelfth century. I once found a moving quotation from Bernard and wanted more. So I went to a larger monastery library to photocopy his commentary and discovered it filled an entire shelf! When Bernard died in 1153, his disciples carried on his work, since The Song of Songs is inexhaustibly rich. One of the best commentaries is by John of the Cross, St. Teresa's partner in the Carmelite Reform. John's poem, "The Spiritual Canticle," is a magnificent reworking of the biblical canticle, and more appealing than his prose commentary on the poem.

Teresa also wrote her own meditations on The Song of Songs, considered scandalous in her day. How could a woman even think these thoughts, let alone commit them to writing? An unenlightened confessor ordered her to burn her commentary. She immediately threw it into the fire, but it had already been copied and was safely in the hands of another convent! We benefit today from the shrewdness of Teresa and her sisters.

As Teresa uses The Song of Songs to describe the prayer of spousal union, she chooses some of the most erotic lines from the Bible:

"Let him kiss me with the kisses of his mouth."
"Your breasts are better than wine and give
   forth the most sweet fragrance."
"His fruit is sweet to my taste."
"He has brought me into the wine-cellar."

These passages manifest the feminine personality: earthy, physical, and sensuous, touching, tasting, and smelling. What does Teresa have to say about the breasts of God, the taste of God, and the experience of entering the wine-cellar?

Breasts, Wine and Kisses

TERESA SPEAKS OFTEN about milk from the breasts of God, masculine breasts. This physical imagery is important and gives us a clue to the enormous mystery of transcendence: how can a woman draw milk from the breasts of a masculine spouse? John of the Cross also talks about this same phenomenon.

The body of God must be taken into account. Teresa casts herself into his arms, kisses his mouth, loses herself in his eyes. She insists that we never abandon the humanity of Christ. We are not angels. We are enfleshed and must therefore relate to an embodied and incarnate God. We may feel squeamish about Christ's body and want our prayer to be exclusively "spiritual," as though such a thing were possible. Even though Jesus was human, we don't like to confront his human body. Teresa thinks we're crazy! She teaches us how the embodiment of Jesus in human flesh can help us pray.

How does God taste? Good! "His fruit is sweet to my taste." According to Teresa, God makes himself into whatever kind of food we need, and gives us himself to eat. Eating is one of the most primordial and intimate human experiences. Look at how often we celebrate love and friendship with a meal. We honor others with a banquet and refer to the next life as "the heavenly banquet." We say to those we love, whether spouse, child, or friend: "I love you so much, I could eat you up." Eating is a sacred act and an expression of profound communion. This is magnificently portrayed in the Danish movie, *Babette's Feast*. Babette helps me understand why the food fights I've seen in both films and real life are more disturbing to me than fist fights.

The Eucharist is the ultimate food God gives us. If we meditate on the Eucharist attentively, instead of in a pious coma, we recognize the ingenious and generous nature of the sacrament. Jesus does not ask us simply to think about him in bloodless mental abstractions. Instead, he offers himself to us in a physical, earthy, embodied way. He says: "You can actually eat me. That's how close you can get." The Eucharist, then, is a vital source and center for Christian spousal prayer.

We may get so carried away in spousal prayer that we walk around like drunkards! According to St. Teresa, God wants us to be totally inebriated. We aren't invited into the divine wine-cellar to sip a little here and there. We're invited to drink every bottle in the cellar so that we become completely God-intoxicated! Can we let go of our inhibitions and go wild? Teresa encourages us not to feel weak or afraid and instead be ready to "die in this paradise of delights."

She writes over and over about happy, holy, heavenly inebriation. But she's as sneaky as our Divine Lover. For eventually she explains why we are given such ecstasy: so that we may be able to bear the agony of life, the crucifying burden of self-sacrificing service. Anyone who walks a spiritual path with integrity will inevitably suffer. God intoxicates us so that we won't know how bad it is when the going gets rough. Teresa makes this comfortingly clear. When we truly love God, we become so captivated that we become more courageous in suffering. Spousal intimacy does not bring us a life of continual bliss but the cross of our Divine Spouse.

Puritanism and Promiscuity

SOME OF US ARE THRILLED to learn about the orthodoxy of spousal prayer because it strikes a resonant chord in our own hearts. Others may squirm uncomfortably considering the mouth and breasts and arms of God. The Song of Songs disconcerts many spiritual people. Ignace Lepp, for example, describes what happened to him when he read passages from the Song in a public gathering:

> *I read from a recent official Catholic translation in which the more obviously erotic expressions had been toned down. The reaction of my listening audience was one of embarrassed silence. They suspected I had read something from Baudelaire or Verlaine* [two of the more ribald French poets], *or perhaps from some "immoral"*

contemporary poet. When I told them it was from the Bible, they hesitated to believe me.

Teresa experienced this herself. She recalls hearing a superb sermon on The Song of Songs in which the priest explained the loving delight with which the soul, as bride, communes with God. The congregation did not understand that this possibility exists for all of us and laughed outright. Teresa was shocked at their attitude.

Spousal prayer is not my own crazy idea. Nor is it merely St. Teresa's personal preference. Spousal prayer lies at the very heart of the Christian mystical tradition. Then why are we so skittish?

We experience discomfort or downright disbelief if we are guilty of "angelism" and neglect or even negate the reality of the body. We may suffer from Cartesian dualism and make a false split between body and spirit. Falling prey to this error, actually considered "heresy" from the Roman Catholic point of view, we may recognize the reality of the body as well as the spirit but insist that they are two separate entities. We may be so puritanical that we find it distasteful enough to consider human spousal intimacy, let alone divine intimacy.

Spousal prayer is also difficult to understand if we suffer at the other extreme from promiscuity. If we are irreverent or too casual about sex, if we consider it merely an adult recreation and lack appreciation for the grandeur and sacramental nature of sex as a gift from the lavish hand of God, we may be disturbed with sexual language used in a spiritual context. We may also feel uncomfortable about spousal prayer if we have no personal experience of it.

Spousal prayer is not easy to discuss. We must do so with discretion and dignity, lest we fall prey to "spiritual voyeurism" or "peeping-Tom mysticism." Teresa calls spousal prayer a deep secret and a great mystery. If we have personal experience, we understand. If we do not have personal experience, we may be confused. But we mustn't be discouraged if we have not yet come to this dimension of intimacy. Whatever divine friendship we enjoy is enriching, provided we do not block off the possibility of newer and deeper realms of experience.

Obstacles to Divine Intimacy

WHAT KEEPS US FROM ENJOYING GOD in a spousal way? Teresa analyzes some of the obstacles and offers us encouragement at every turn.

A false sense of unworthiness may hold us back. "Who am I?" we ask. "How could someone like me possibly know God this way?" Yet all God asks is humility of heart: "The humble contrite heart you will not spurn, O Lord" (Psalm 51:19). No one talks about the necessity and power of humility more than St. Teresa, but when it comes to spousal prayer, she clearly states that this is not a time to get bogged down by personal guilt. If we focus on our unworthiness, we will not be able to accept the gift of intimacy God offers. We may feel unworthy or undeserving, but that is beside the point. What matters now is the incredible overture of love the Holy One is making. Refusing to respond is not humility, but what Teresa calls faint-heartedness and false pride. When we are truly humble, we do not refuse God's gift but gratefully accept it the way we accept a human gift. We say, "Thank you!" We say, "Yes!" Then we enjoy the gift.

Fear is another impediment. Prayer may sometimes seem frightening. As McNamara says, "God is not nice: not a buddy nor an uncle nor a mascot; God is an earthquake." Who knows what will happen when we enter the love-chamber to meet our Divine Spouse? "Do not be anxious," says Teresa, to help relieve us of our neurotic fear. "Do not be afraid when God favors you in this way."

We will never know God spousally if we think this prayer is impossible, improper, or unimportant. Even if we accept the reality of spousal prayer in general, we may preclude it by saying, "But it's not for me." For many years I believed that this particular kind of prayer was not meant for everyone. But St. Teresa has convinced me of the opposite. She insists that everyone is called to this prayer to some degree or another, at one time or another.

May nothing hinder us from begging God for this intimate friendship. We need ardent desire and what Teresa calls "holy daring." She chides us for being content with so little. God wants to give us absolutely everything. Why do we settle for less? Why do we remain at the foot of the mountain instead of climbing all the way to the top?

Teresa is deeply disturbed that so many of us settle for less and is intensely eager for us to pray this way. Peppering her pages with multiple "Ohs" and exclamation points, she cries out: "Oh, oh! What's the matter with you? Why are you so blind? Why do you hold back?" Then she catches herself, calms down, and says, "Oh! What have I done? Pardon me." That is why her writing is so refreshing: she is not methodical and dry but spontaneous, as if she were standing in front of us, carrying on an impassioned conversation.

Madness and Reason

THE BIGGEST OBSTACLE to divine intimacy is too much common sense. Teresa is called the "saint of common sense" and rightly so. She highly prized this quality, but she also knew the danger of an overdose. If we are excessively sensible, we will never be able to let go enough to be intoxicated by God, who often "seizes" us beyond reason, the way a great lover "takes" the beloved. We've got to go out of our minds to pray spousally and become so enkindled with love that we go "mad!"

Teresa prized study and learning. Before she made major decisions, she always consulted "learned men," her term for the theologians of her day. But when it came to spousal prayer, she sometimes took command. She became so frustrated when these mentors were excessively sensible and held her back that she penned some of her most vehement and satirical passages about this problem. I like to read them aloud in my hermitage, the way Teresa probably said them herself. "Hearing" her speak makes her thinking come more alive.

Catch the fire in her voice as she says: *"Some* learned men whom the Lord does not lead by this mode of prayer, and who haven't even *begun* a life of prayer, want to be *so rational* about things, and *so precise* in their understanding" (italics mine). When we reach this realm of prayer, we may run into difficulty with spiritual guidance, the way Teresa did. We need sound spiritual counsel, yet not allow anyone to tell us we're crazy or that we should have nothing to do with this kind of prayer.

Teresa valued reason but staunchly criticized excessive rationality. Many of us get stuck in a low level of prayer Teresa describes in the Third Mansion of *The Interior Castle*. On this level, we experience very little real agony or ecstasy in either prayer or life because we are too reasonable, routine, upright and orderly. Our lives must indeed be ordered and deliberate, not haphazard. This is a crucial first step in spiritual development. But if we make an ordered life the final step, and guard it as an end in itself, we never grow into the heights and depths Teresa describes so masterfully because our reason is still very much in control. Teresa feels tremendous sorrow and compassion for those stuck in this rut and says: "Love has not yet reached the point of overwhelming reason. But I would like us to use our reason to make us dissatisfied with being so reasonable." What a liberating challenge: to use reason to undo reason! Why proceed merely step-by-step like a toad or a fettered chicken (Teresa's images)? Why not leap? Make the journey all at once? Soar like an eagle?

Social Ramifications

REDISCOVERING THE MEANING of sublimation and spousal prayer has enormous social consequences in an era such as ours when love, marriage, and celibacy are undermined by infidelity, codependency, sexual addiction, and a moral relativism that may lead to moral chaos.

If we understood the tremendous value and beauty of spousal prayer and nurtured it, celibate men and women might be more sexually fulfilled through healthy sublimation. Married men and women might stop expecting their spouses to be God as well as mate, financial partner and co-parent, romantic love object and red hot lover, best friend and fitness coach, "home-repair person" and "scintillating companion through the wasteland of Sunday afternoons."

This negative perception of the Sabbath is particularly tragic and telling. It comes from a magazine essay explaining how Americans expect marriage to be "a micro-Utopia on Earth." In its attitude towards Sunday, marriage, and the "marriage-saving concept" of the "discreet, long-term, European style affair," this essay demonstrates our spiritual bankruptcy. As a culture we may well have only two choices: mysticism or neurosis, sublimation or sexual chaos, spousal prayer or social upheaval. May we pray with St. Teresa:

Who could explain the benefit that lies in throwing ourselves into the arms of this Lord of ours and making an agreement with His Majesty that I look at my Beloved and my Beloved at me... Let Him kiss me with the kiss of His mouth, for without You, what am I, Lord? If I am not close to you, what am I worth? If I stray a little from Your Majesty, where will I end up? Oh, my Lord, my Mercy, and my Good! And what greater good could I want in this life than to be close to You, that there be no division between You and me? With this companionship, what can be difficult? What can one not undertake for You, being so closely joined?

Tessa in her monastic years, at the walls of Avila, 1990.

CONVERSATION FOUR
Love-wounds and Service

THE FIRST CONSEQUENCE of prayer, then, is *espousal.* As Swiss theologian Hans Urs von Balthasar wrote: "God has set up in the middle of the history of humanity, with all its terrors and hells, a marriage bed, splendid and untouchable. It is portrayed in The Song of Songs."

This divine love may take years to grow, like any human love, allowing for those exceptions when we may be swept off our feet in a flaming instant! Teresa uses the various stages in human courtship to describe the stages of prayer. First we meet, exchange gifts and get acquainted. Eventually we are betrothed, and then finally we marry. True love deepens and grows gradually, over a lifetime. As the prophet Hosea teaches: "I will allure her: I will lead her into the desert and speak to her heart.... I will espouse you to me forever" (Hosea 2:16, 21).

Generous Service

BUT THE MATTER does not end here. Another consequence of prayer is far more demanding: generous, self-spending, and exhausting *service.* Teresa even uses the word "laborious." The proper relationship between these two consequences is clear in the teachings of Jesus. First, he says, "Love the Lord your God with all your mind and heart and soul and body." *Espousal.* Second, "Love your neighbor as yourself." *Service.*

We are called to leave that splendid marriage bed and face humanity's "terrors and hells," or sometimes worse, the tedious and mundane details of being human. When we initially learn about spousal prayer, we are tempted to think that prayer will always be "bed-chamber ecstasy." It certainly was a rude awakening for me when I realized that my intimacy with God would leave me regularly exhausted from the demands of laborious service: voluminous correspondence, extensive travel, hard manual labor, hours of talk and counseling, and worst of all, being chained to a desk with the unending details and burdens of administration. This is so similar to married love. How much time do husbands and wives actually spend enjoying bed-chamber ecstasy? More of their time is spent in mutual service of one another, their families, and their extended community, often extending to the whole planet. The same is true in our love-life with the Divine.

We cannot expect to remain forever in a state of delight and may need to challenge those who proclaim they always enjoy the ecstasy of spousal prayer. Continual ecstasy is not possible or even advisable. The honeymoon period does not last forever. Teresa's conclusion is more realistic. She meditates on The Song of Songs extensively and ecstatically and then finishes with an ecstatic description of laborious service:

Perhaps it will seem to them... that to remain in a corner enjoying this delight is what is important. These beginners do not understand... the Lord will take care, when they are strong, to bring them further.... The more they advance in this kind of prayer and the gifts of our Lord, the more attention they pay to the needs of their neighbor.... Much good is done by those who, after speaking with His Majesty for several years, when receiving His gifts and delights, want to serve in laborious ways even though these delights and consolations are thereby hindered.

The tenor of our prayer changes in its later stages. At first we want only the experience of delight. This can be an attempt to escape from reality. As our prayer grows deeper and more authentic, we want to spend ourselves serving God and the world created out of divine love. Towards that end, we gladly sacrifice our own consolation.

The Freedom of Slavery

THE SECOND CONSEQUENCE of prayer is not merely service, however laborious. Teresa actually uses the word "slavery," in a mysteriously liberating sense. "Do you know what it means to be spiritual?" she asks. We can easily substitute "espoused" for spiritual: "It means becoming the slaves of God. Marked with His brand, which is that of the cross, spiritual persons, because now they have given Him their liberty, can be sold by Him as slaves of everyone, as He was." This sums up the essence of Teresa's mysticism. The generous and holy woman then goes on to say that if we are not determined to become Christ's slaves, we aren't making progress.

Slaves? Branded with the sign of the cross? Such vehement language may confuse or even repel us. But it demands a strong response. How often do we approach the sign of the cross mechanically and mindlessly, unaware of its radical implications? In one of the most powerful liturgies I ever celebrated in monastic community, Father William traced the sign of the cross on our backs with a sword as we lay prostrate in prayer on the floor of the chapel in Nova Scotia. Since I am not only fond of the chivalric Christ but also the "Cowboy Christ," I often thought of my monastic life as "riding for the brand." It was light-hearted and almost flippant, but I was deeply aware of the real meaning: like Teresa, I was marked with Christ's brand and became the "slave" of everyone, as he was.

As a sign of spiritual matrimony, some mystics have "received" a wedding ring from their Divine Spouse. According to some sources, St. Catherine of Sienna was given one made of magnificent jewels. But Catherine herself said it was made of the circumcised flesh of the Infant Jesus! As if to "compete" with Catherine, who predated Teresa by two hundred years, some Teresian enthusiasts claimed Teresa received an amethyst ring. This testimony is printed in most anthologies, but not accepted by those heroic enough to embrace Teresa's sterner account of her wedding gift. This woman, already pierced by a flaming arrow, now branded with the cross and sold as a slave, received a nail, symbol of her own crucifixion. Her account of the moment is moving:

*He gave me His right hand and said: "Behold this nail;
it is a sign you will be My bride from today on. Until now
you have not merited this; from now on not only will you
look after My honor as being the honor of your Creator,
King, and God, but you will look after it as My true bride.
My honor is yours, and yours Mine.*

Teresa's prayer was filled with ecstasy, rapture, and
swoons of delight. Yet she ended up enslaved, suffering, and
on the cross. This is the ultimate ecstasy: to be crucified with
the Beloved Spouse.

Mystery of the Cross

I GREW UP HEARING that the cross is the gift God gives to
friends. But if we truly love God, do we wait for the gift of
the cross or climb up there ourselves? If the cross is where
God is, then we also belong there. This is why the traditional
Carmelite cross has no corpus: the cross is not merely a
memorial, but a challenge. By meditating on a bare cross,
we recognize that we ourselves must be crucified on it. The
cross in my own oratory does have a corpus on it, as large and
graphically human as I can find. I appreciate the barrenness
of the Carmelite cross, but the brute challenge of it doesn't
motivate me. As a woman and a lover, however, I am moved
by the sight of my Beloved. Where he is, I want to be. What
he suffers, I want to share. Who he is, I want to be: crucified
for love. I sometimes hold my crucifix when I pray, weeping in
desperate agony or stunned silent in my pain, laughing in the
joy of intimacy or bowed low, in the awe of adoration. (We

say "I adore you!" to our human loves. Why not proclaim it to our Divine Love?)

The choice of a crucifix is not easy. Not much Christian art appeals to me. No wonder we seldom hang crucifixes in our homes and schools. Sometimes we don't even hang them in our churches. Over the years, my community, the Spiritual Life Institute, designed deeply inspiring and artistic crucifixes.

The crucifix on my oratory wall is my favorite because I know it with such fierce intimacy. The corpus is exquisitely carved out of blond wood. It is all the more meaningful because for many years we carried it in our processions during Holy Week, from Palm Sunday to Holy Saturday. On Good Friday we "venerated" it, draped in blood red cloth or the purple of penance and mourning. We fell to our knees and kissed the feet of Jesus. I still feel the weight of each one's joy and sorrow when I look at this crucifix, and this heightens my prayer of intercession.

The crucifix suspended in mid-air over the stark stone altar in the Sangre de Cristo Chapel in Crestone, Colorado is an evocation of heroic, human-divine eros. It portrays the seemingly impossible reconciliation of love and death in an act of absolute freedom. The body of Christ is both bronze and wood to suggest the humanity and divinity of Jesus. Christ's flesh was truly material and mortal and participated in the cosmos. In this masterful work of art, his body is not merely on the cross; his body *is* the cross.

Because of his divinity, Christ's body passed through the crucible of crucifixion and rose in radiant vitality from the tomb. I get the chills when I hear this marvel proclaimed on

Easter morning. As Mary Magdalene and the other women weep around the empty tomb, the angel comforts them with almost a rebuke: "Why do you search for the Living One among the dead?"

The artist who created this crucifix, Dan Davidson from Santa Fe, New Mexico, portrays the dying Jesus, not the dead man. In the powerful act of dying, Jesus' gaze pierces beyond death. His eyes are open, not closed. He peers upward, not merely in anguish, but also in awed, astonished recognition of the Father's face. In his life on earth, Jesus was never one to dally, and here, in death, he is too divinely impatient for resignation. He is ready to swallow death whole. (As St. Paul cried out, "Oh death, where is your victory? Oh death, where is your sting?") He presses upward, as if to leap into the Resurrection of Easter morning.

The face of Jesus is universal, and we all see it differently. But many people meditate on the one in this crucifix and say, "Yes, this is how Jesus must have looked." The face shows not only simultaneous strength and vulnerability, but also luminosity, shining out of the very heart of pain.

The crucifix in our chapel in Nova Scotia was controversial because Christ wore no loincloth. His naked penis, circumcised according to Jewish tradition, hung in full view. Some secular historians say that Christ was hung on the gibbet naked. Some of the Fathers of the Church agree: Augustine, Ambrose, Ephraim, Cyril, John Chrysostom. We must not hide the disgrace Jesus bore with such magnificent absurdity on the cross. Hanging there naked, he revealed the naked truth in all its splendor. I sometimes find nudity silly. But the naked Christ is utterly serious, revealing the bare truth about us: We are incarnational beings. We cannot mentally "prove" the existence of God because we are not mere minds. But we can embody God in our lives because of our flesh, in union with Jesus, the Word, who became flesh and dwelt among us.

Teresa does not mention any particular crucifix in her writings. She loved a statue of Christ scourged at the pillar and was fond of paintings of Jesus, sometimes using her last coins to purchase them. At one time she was concerned that this was against the spirit of poverty. But in her prayer she came to understand that it was far better to be loving than poor and said: "I shouldn't renounce anything that awakens my love." This is sound spiritual wisdom, when we are called to transfigure, not reject matter.

Deeper Meanings

THERE ARE MANY WAYS to interpret the deeper spiritual significance of the cross. Purification of the ego is major. Those who repudiate the cross of Christ and then do spiritual practices with a dagger to "kill ego" have missed the crux of the matter.

It is important to recognize the cosmic implications of the crucifixion. The stained glass windows I helped envision in the Spiritual Life Institute's Colorado chapel show how the earth itself is crucified, symbolized by a barren tree. The windows also show the crucifixion of the animal kingdom, both wild and domesticated. Animal crucifixions provide some of my most stirring meditations: Marc Chagall's painting of the flayed ox, for example. I meditate on this every Lent, along with others I've collected over the years: the Auschwitz Christ in his blue and white striped uniform, the Atomic Christ, blackened and burned, and the crucified lion on Father Dave Denny's ordination invitation.

It helps to personalize the crucifixion. How can we enter into this clearly historical event deeply enough to penetrate its trans-historical, trans-denominational, trans-cultural significance? Three of my friends have done this remarkably well. Sharon Doyle, whose heritage is Scotch-Irish, designed a Celtic cross which forms the crossbars of a window. Through this cross-window we are led into eternity, where we play in yellow fields, a potent and childlike symbol of the resurrected order of being. Songwriter Tom Renaud added a Celtic harp and star of hope to his sword-cross and wrote:

> *He bids me bear the harp and play*
> *While the dark night rages on.*
> *He bids me bear His sword and rise*
> *With the Morning Star at dawn.*

Father Dave Denny, like Miguel de Unamuno imbued with a tragic sense of life, uses the fiddle, with Christ stretched cruciform on its bow and strings. Since he paradoxically honors Lord Buddha as one of the major inspirations behind his conversion to Catholicism, Dave has another cross with Buddha on it. This is not a personal whim but an ancient symbol used by sixteenth-century Japanese Catholics when they were being persecuted by the ruling Buddhists.

In our own day, Buddhists and Hindus have contributed profound insights into the meaning of the cross. Thich Nhat Hanh, the Vietnamese Zen monk who has worked so hard for peace of soul within his country and ours since the Vietnam War, teaches us to awaken to the reality of suffering in the world. Mahatma Gandhi called the crucifixion of Jesus "a perfect act." Gandhi loved to sing Christian hymns and made them familiar in India beyond the bounds of Christian churches. One of his favorites conveys the universal significance of the cross.

I once spoke at an inter-spiritual gathering where I was frequently challenged by former Christians who had turned to Eastern practices. One particularly hostile participant tried to trap the Dalai Lama into declaring that the Christian cross leads to masochistic wallowing in suffering. Knowing that this is an aberration which may be found in Buddhism as well as Christianity, His Holiness refused to be ensnared, and responded: "The only way out of suffering is through it." Buddha on the cross with Jesus. Tibetan Buddhism crucified by the Chinese Communists the way Soviet Communists crucified Christianity. The Dalai Lama called His Holiness, the same reverential title Catholics use to address the Pope. East meets West when we understand the cross in depth.

Swords of Sorrow, Swords of Joy

THE DEEPEST MEANING of the cross is love, as we see from saints and sages both East and West. To live is to love, and to love is to suffer in many ways: from misunderstanding and relentless responsibilities, from bad health, opposition and abandonment, from emotional abuse and unrequited or even rejected love. We keenly feel the wounds of human love. We may feel the wounds of love even more in our intimacy with Christ, a True Friend and Lover. With St. Teresa, our love of God may increase so powerfully that it becomes unbearable. We can't stop thinking about our Beloved and voicing "loving complaints." This growing love may be described as an awakening or an impulse, a touch or a wound. "The wound causes a severe pain which makes the soul moan," Teresa says, "yet the pain is so delightful the soul would never want it to go away."

Teresa distinguishes mature intense passion from immature exaggerated devotional feelings. In the latter instance, she teaches, we are like a pot boiling over on the stove, or children crying so furiously that they are about to suffocate. Their excessive emotions cease when they are finally given something to drink. This lower level of disquiet is very sensory, linked to natural weakness, and should be held in check by a gentle use of reason.

Higher impulses or deeper wounds of love are far different from exterior feelings and sensory delights. They are not felt where earthly sufferings are felt, but in a very deep and intimate part of the "soul." These wounds are so delicate and refined that even St. Teresa can't find fitting comparisons to describe them. Yet the images she chooses are vivid and compelling. The awakenings of love come as quickly and unexpectedly as a thunderclap or a blazing comet. The soul feels wounded in an exquisite manner, as though pierced simultaneously by a sword of sorrow and a sword of joy. Teresa maintains that the feelings of the soul are much more severe than those of the body. In the presence of this spiritual pain, we hardly feel physical pain.

Flaming Arrows

WHEN TERESA WAS FORTY-FIVE and alone at prayer in her room, she felt as though a flaming arrow had been thrust deep into the living recesses of her heart by a magnificent angel. She could not understand how such pain and glory could be combined; but she clasped the suffering close to her, for this experience of "transverberation" was glorious.

> *I saw in his hands a large golden dart and at the end of the iron tip there appeared to be a little fire. It seemed to me this angel plunged the dart several times into my heart and that it reached deep within me. When he drew it out, I thought he was carrying off with him the deepest part of me; and he left me all on fire with great love of God. The pain was so great that it made me moan, and the sweetness this greatest pain caused me was so superabundant that there is no desire capable of taking it away; nor is the soul content with less than God. The pain is not bodily but spiritual, although the body doesn't fail to share in some of it, and even a great deal. The loving exchange that takes place between the soul and God is so sweet that I beg Him in His goodness to give a taste of this love to anyone who thinks I am lying.*

This instance was particularly dramatic, but throughout her life, in moments of both agony and ecstasy, Teresa felt the transpiercing of her soul. This deeply interior experience does not occur in a vacuum, but often in relation to some natural human experience. We find a good example of this in Teresa's twelfth *Spiritual Testimony*.

It was the Easter season, but Teresa was far from feeling the joy of the Resurrection. She was lonely. Her spiritual director and friend, Martín Gutiérrez, had left her quickly the day before. She understood that this Jesuit rector in Salamanca was a busy man, but she needed him, and his hasty departure left her afflicted and fragile. When Isabel de Jesús Jimena sang a little song about how hard it is to endure life without God, Teresa felt greater affliction than ever and even cried out aloud as she felt the transpiercing of her soul. Her body was wracked by it; the next day she felt painfully disjointed.

This growing love of God makes us suffer because we feel our distance from the Divine. It seems as though a spark from the conflagration of God's love falls upon us, making us burn. But the spark goes out too soon and we are overwhelmed with desire to be utterly consumed by the Fire. This experience is not an isolated one; as in all genuine mysticism, it leaves powerful effects. In this case, we are full of determination to suffer and to withdraw from every distracting conversation and consolation.

These impulses of love continue to escalate until they reach a passionate longing that becomes so intense, Teresa compares it to an arduous martyrdom and the death agony. "I was dying with desire to see God," she wrote in her *Life*, "and I didn't know where to seek this life except in death. Some great impulses of this love came upon me... I didn't know what to do with myself. For nothing satisfied me, nor could I put up with myself." This deep pain indicates a high level of growth, a final purification, like gold in the crucible, before we enter the Seventh Mansion, Teresa's image for the highest grace in life: union with God in mystical marriage.

In this purging pain we experience a strange and extreme sense of solitude because nothing on earth consoles us, and no one provides us company. We feel lost in the middle of a desert, crucified between heaven and earth, as though we were suffocating with a rope around our necks. Yet the torment is pleasing and seems safer because it follows the way of the cross. Teresa esteemed it more than all her other graces. Though this pain makes it more difficult for us to return to everyday life, Teresa encourages us to surrender to it. Through the suffering of these wounds of love, we finally sprout wings and learn to fly with ease. And we finally give up our self-will and our egotism.

Long to Die, Live to Serve

IN THE EXPERIENCE of human love, we agonize over the absence of the beloved, as we see in Teresa's friendship with Gutiérrez, and even more so with her other close friends, Jerónimo Gracián and Maria de San José. The same is true in our relationship to God. When our love for the Divine grows strong enough, we are filled with desire to be united more intimately. Knowing how limited this is before death, we may long to die. Teresa bitterly laments in one of her poems:

Only with that surety
I will die do I live,
Because in dying
My hope in living is assured.
Death, bringing life,
Do not tarry; I await you.
I die because I do not die.

See how love is strong.
Life, do not trouble me.
See how all that remains
Is in losing you to gain.
Come now, sweet death,
Come, dying swiftly.
I die because I do not die.

Teresa was in this stage by the time she finished writing her *Life*. But then she grew still more, and in the midst of her longings to die, she experienced great willingness to go on living longer in order to serve more generously. This self-sacrifice is the highest degree of prayer. "See me here, Lord," we must pray with Teresa: "If it's necessary to live in order to render You some service, I don't refuse all the trials that can come to me on earth." We find this conviction echoing over and over again throughout Teresa's writings, reaching truly heroic proportions in the Seventh Mansion.

Longing for death does not deaden but heightens our compassion for this world. Wounds of love lead us to deep concern for those we love: family, friends, enemies, the society in which we live, the earth under our feet. This loving concern brings us to the prayer of intercession for those we cherish, and this in turn leads to deeper wounding. We experience painful concern for the physical well-being of those we love, and even more for their spiritual well-being. Teresa was particularly concerned about world rulers with insufficient understanding of their deepest spiritual obligations.

Before we reach this level, we don't care very much about anything but ourselves. As we grow, we find ourselves in the midst of painful concerns. We recognize others as children of the Divine, our brothers and sisters, and the grief we feel for them breaks and grinds our souls to pieces. This grief results from union with Christ, suffering over the broken world, who died not so much from flesh wounds but a broken heart. We have been brought into the inner wine cellar and sealed with a divine seal, which is to suffer out of love. The ardor of this love outweighs any suffering we may undergo, for suffering comes to an end, but love is forever.

CONVERSATION FIVE
Meeting the Beloved

PRAYER IS A SPONTANEOUS human act as natural as breathing and as necessary. Prayer is to the human heart what breath is to the body. As Danish philosopher Søren Kierkegaard said, "If we don't breathe, we die. If we don't pray, we die spiritually."

Christian prayer is a vast realm of experience that ranges from the verbal recitation of ready-made prayers to the affective dimensions of spousal prayer and the highest stages of contemplation without words, thoughts, or props of any kind. When we consider prayer in the Christian tradition, we mean many variations. We mean the old lady in the church pew, fingering her rosary beads, or mumbling the same prayer she has read for years from her dog-eared prayer book, bound together by a rubber band. We mean the tired young mother who has no time, heaving a heavy sigh and falling asleep in the living room chair as she offers up her exhausting day as prayer. We mean the silence of monks and nuns as they pore over the scriptures in their monastery libraries or sit in quiet contemplation in their cells. We mean the ethereal sound of Gregorian chant rising from a lavish liturgical celebration at St. Peter's basilica in Rome or the inarticulate groans that pour from hospital beds, dirty hovels, and the anguished soul of John Paul II in his private chapel. (Many observers reported the self-oblivious passion of the Pope's prayer. I am particularly devoted to this new saint.)

Many disaffected Christians left the institutional Church when they were on the level of Sunday school rote prayers. Turning East, they learned sophisticated levels of Transcendental, Vipassana, Tibetan, or Zen Buddhist meditation. Never having the opportunity to explore the same levels within Christianity, they remain unaware of its rich mystical resources: St. Teresa and her bridal mysticism, St. Ignatius and his spiritual exercises, *The Cloud of Unknowing* and its "naked intent directed unto God." Nor are they aware of the work of many contemporary teachers, Thomas Keating and his "centering prayer," John Main and his fellowship of Christian meditation, or William McNamara's "earthy mysticism," reminiscent of the Celtic tradition.

St. John Damascene, the last of the Greek Fathers of the Church, explains prayer as *a raising of the mind and heart to God.* McNamara calls it *a cry of the heart,* insisting that contemplation is for everyone: "The contemplative is not a special kind of person. Everyone is, or ought to be, a special kind of contemplative." Teresa describes prayer as an *"intimate sharing between friends."* If prayer is friendship with God, then the same lessons which apply to friendship between human persons also apply here. Good friendship means making time to be alone with the one we love who also loves us.

In this sense, prayer is not an exercise but an encounter, not a practice but a presence, not a technique, but meeting the Beloved. We need to ask the "how to" questions, but they cannot be answered with mechanics. Prayer is more readily caught than taught. We cannot stage it, but we can set the stage. We cannot control it, but we can create the climate for it.

Preparation and Reading

A REVERED OLD Christian tradition describes prayer in rhythmic and rhyming Latin: *lectio, meditatio, oratio,* and *contemplatio,* which mean reading, meditation, prayer, and contemplation. To these four classical stages I like to add two more (not exactly in correct Latin!): *preparatio* before we begin and *operatio* (overflowing action) at the end. All these stages may be called prayer.

Many problems in prayer are due to a lack of adequate preparation. We must ready ourselves for any formal period of prayer by making the transition away from our ordinary workaday mode. I was trained to call this "PPP": "proximate preparation for prayer," that is, what I do for the hour prior to a formal period of prayer.

There are various ways to prepare in order to become more mindful, focused, attentive, wakeful, or "recollected," which is the time-honored Catholic term. I favor physical and poetic activities which demand enough energy to engage the whole mind and narrow our focus to what my favorite Zen roshi calls "just this." I love to walk or swim, stack wood, weed the garden, or turn the compost. Since much of the work I do each day is at my desk, using my body before prayer both rests my weary mind and wakes it up to new possibilities. It's also helpful to listen to good music, look at (or create) a piece of art, concentrate on the breath, a burning candle, or the sunset.

The Western spiritual tradition has always found good reading a powerful preparation for prayer. When the ancients taught *lectio,* they originally meant the reading of sacred scripture. This requires tremendous imagination. We must get beyond the words by immersion in the Word and place ourselves inside the scripture, making it our own personal experience.

My own favorite scriptural scene takes place sometime after the Resurrection, when the disciples discover Jesus cooking fish on the beach. John the Evangelist reveals the homey details: the charcoal fire, Peter's nakedness, and an astounding 153 fish. There is radical simplicity here. Jesus rose from the dead and burst out of the tomb in something akin to an atomic explosion! And what does he say to his followers? "Come and have breakfast." No matter how often I meditate on this passage, I am filled with wonder.

As Christian spirituality evolved through the centuries, *lectio* came to include other spiritual reading besides scripture. I recommend reading broadly in the worlds of art, literature, poetry, science, myth, comparative religion, and what Teresa called "the book of nature," for God "speaks" to us in many different ways. "Everything in this world is either a sign or a sample or a symbol of God," William McNamara insists. "The universe is diaphanous. The world is crammed with God. In every person or event met prayerfully, there is an overriding, transcendent, unconditional character that is captured in these words of the prophet, 'Thus saith the Lord.' In every situation the man or woman of prayer is aware of being addressed, claimed, and sustained."

Since the focus of this book is spousal prayer, the most conducive *lectio* might be drawn from the rich tradition of bridal mysticism. It helps to read good Christ books or look at good Christ art, since the Christian should always be feasting on the life of Christ. Christian wisdom initially came to us as story. Whenever the story fades, we become distracted by peripheral issues. In losing the story, we lose the glory. We transform an exciting story into a dull system. If we tell and retell the Christ-story, we may recover our own story.

Reading is appropriate preparation for prayer only when it is meditative. This means an exercise of the whole mind which includes not only our mental faculties but also our emotional, intuitive, and even visceral ones. The mind must sink into the heart, and the heart must catch fire. So should the belly! Reading meditatively means reading slowly and reflectively, ruminating on a few words instead of covering a vast number of pages. In this way, *lectio* flows naturally into *meditatio*.

Meditation Practices

One meditation practice which evolved spontaneously in my life uses scripture as a springboard for spousal intimacy with Christ. I call it the "How was your day?" practice. I imagine that my Divine Spouse and I have met at the end of a busy day. We were physically apart from one another for hours, yet I lived each hour in his presence, more or less. Now we meet again "face-to-face." We talk and touch and share our joys and burdens. I tell him about my day. This is a natural opportunity to review my life, to make an "examination of conscience," to assess the quality of my day and my own responsibility for a "good" or "bad" one. Then I ask my Beloved, "And how was your day?" Using some incident from the Gospels, I let Jesus "tell" me about it. I listen carefully to what he has to "say" as he shares thoughts and feelings, doubts and fears, joys and jokes. (Yes, Jesus did joke, in the grand Middle Eastern style, full of irony, wit and satirical storytelling.)

This kind of meditation focuses on the historical Christ. Another focuses on the mystical and cosmic Christ. Gazing at the glowing embers in a fire pit outside my hermitage, I meditate on Christ as the Living Flame who said he came to cast fire on the earth. Facing the mountains in the snow on an icy January morning, I watch the sun rise and greet him as the "Radiant Dawn," using one of the exquisite "Oh Antiphons" we pray during the last seven days before Christmas. Diving into the lake in the heat of summer, I swim in the same Living Water that turns into a spring inside me, "welling up to eternal life," as Jesus revealed to the Samaritan woman.

Breathing is also a Christian meditation practice. We use short prayers we call "aspirations" or "breaths," because prayer is as natural and necessary as our breathing. These aspirations are similar to Hindu or Buddhist mantras. Some are ancient traditions such as the Jesus prayer: "Lord Jesus Christ, have mercy on me, a sinner." In order to pray this more rhythmically while

I walk or exercise, I drop the extra syllables to make an even four-count: "Lord Jesus Christ, have mercy on me." I've prayed this so many years through so many leg lifts and sit-ups that I automatically pray it when I'm not focused on anything in particular.

If we cultivate a listening heart, we will hear the aspirations given to us by the Holy Spirit. They often change, depending on what we need for our spiritual growth. At one time in my life, my aspiration was "Blessed be Jesus in the most holy sacrament of the altar," which comes from a favorite ritual known as Benediction. During a season of dramatic conversion, it was a line from Francis Thompson's poem, "The Hound of Heaven": "Naked I await Thy love's uplifted stroke." I repeated the words over and over until they became my very breath, until I became naked, waiting for the uplifted stroke of love. More recently, when I saturated myself in the works of St. Teresa, I found myself breathing these lines from her poetry: "I am thine, I was born for Thee, what dost Thou want of me?"

See how fluidly we have moved from *lectio* and even *preparatio* into *meditatio* and then *oratio* or prayer. We can make clear demarcations between these stages only at the beginning, in our halting self-conscious efforts to pray. Later, as our prayer deepens, it's difficult to separate one movement from another because each flows naturally into the next and back again. This becomes even truer as we move from meditation to contemplation.

From Meditation to Contemplation

IT HELPS TO DISTINGUISH between meditation and contemplation, especially in an era when East is meeting West. I remember my first years in Buddhist-Christian dialogue. I pleaded for a clarification of terms, but the sponsors of the conference would not hear of it. They conceded only three years later after much confusion, frustration, and misunderstanding. As it turned out, when I said meditation, the Theravadan teachers thought I meant what they call contemplation. When I said contemplation, it meant meditation to them.

From the Christian point of view, meditation is a preparatory act, a mindfulness practice, the concentration or recollection of our scattered faculties. Contemplation is the fruit of meditation, an experiential awareness, insight, and intuition. Meditation is active, contemplation is passive, that is, receptive and responsive. Not a limp passivity, as if we were stretched out in the street, waiting to be run over by a bulldozer, but a wise passiveness, alert, alive and awake. The contemplative moment then unfolds as simple experiential awareness of the real and grows deeply into loving experiential awareness of The Real. John of the Cross gives a beautiful example of contemplative spousal prayer in his poem, "The Dark Night":

> *I abandoned and forgot myself,*
> *Laying my face on my Beloved,*
> *All things ceased; I went out from myself,*
> *Leaving my cares*
> *Forgotten among the lilies.*

A contemporary Baptist minister puts it this way: "I reads myself full, I thinks myself clear, I prays myself hot, and I lets myself go!"

St. Teresa says that meditation is like the laborious process of drawing water from a well, and contemplation is being drenched with rain. St. Francis de Sales compares meditation to eating because we have to work at it. He compares contemplation to drinking because it simply flows. In a more contemporary example, William McNamara uses the image of surfing on the California coast. Meditation is preparing the way: waking up early, going down to the beach, waxing the board, and paddling out to sea, in other words, being there. Contemplation is riding the big wave! This metaphor is particularly helpful, because the secret to good surfing is the secret to genuine contemplation: waiting, and waiting, and more waiting.

If we restrict our prayer to the meditation stage and never stop "working," our prayer is stunted and never really soars into higher realms. At the beginning, meditation dominates. In later stages, we may not even need the preliminary meditation. As the Buddhists say, "If you get to the other shore, you don't need the raft anymore." Or as John of the Cross pointed out so humorously: "If you find the orange peeled, eat it."

In *The Ascent of Mount Carmel,* this Mystical Doctor of the Church gives us three signs to help us discern whether it is time to stop meditating and move into contemplation, or whether we are simply lazy and want to escape the discipline of meditation. 1.) We cannot meditate easily any longer. Our reason and imagination no longer "work." 2.)

We experience no consolation from God, or from anything else. Our imagination is restless and cannot focus on the Divine. Nor will it focus anywhere else. 3.) We find ourselves drawn lovingly and irresistibly to God, but obscurely. We enjoy being alone in the divine presence, but this presence becomes darker and more vague. Deep peace alternates with painful distraction and aridity, that is, we no longer "feel" God. Eventually the quiet peace predominates. All three of these signs must be present simultaneously. No single one is a signal to stop meditation.

Time, Space and Touchstones

WE CAN PRAY any time and all the time, but the discipline of regularly scheduled prayer time is helpful. Those who claim to "pray always" but never pray formally may be misguided. Some of us pray better in the morning, some in the evening, some at noon or in the middle of the night. We all need to find the "right" time and be faithful to it, changing it from time to time when our prayer goes stale. St. Teresa recommends two periods of prayer daily, morning and evening.

We can pray anywhere and everywhere, but special places help. Some pray better indoors, some outside in nature. Some prefer to pray in familiar surroundings: the living room or the bedroom. Others need to set aside a special place. I'm always impressed by how many of my Tibetan Buddhist friends create shrine rooms in their homes. Only a few of my Christian friends are this committed. It is unfortunate that we seldom hang crucifixes and religious art on our walls any more. These "sacramentals" help remind us that every moment of life has a sacramental dimension.

We need to find the best place to pray and be faithful to it, changing it occasionally, like our prayer time, when we go stale. And we need to be creative about our prayer places. I love to pray lying on the beach, paddling a canoe in the moonlight, or walking at twilight. I always pray outside at sunrise and in bed before I go to sleep. Lighting a candle helps set the stage, as does burning incense and playing music. I love praying in front of my crucifix or Salvador Dali's painting, "Christ of St. John of the Cross." Facing a dresser is deadly, especially if it has a mirror. Portable TVs and computers in bedrooms have spoiled both lovemaking between husbands and wives and the lovemaking of spousal prayer.

Sometimes a small touchstone helps. Mine have included a shell from a California beach where I experienced a major turning point in my life, a rock from the walls of St. Teresa's Avila, a clay figurine of Gandalf the Grey (J.R.R. Tolkien's remarkable wizard, who vividly represents the resurrected Christ to me), an oak leaf to connect me with my Celtic ancestors, and a pomegranate, a medieval symbol of the Mystical Body of Christ and a reminder of all the poetry life has to offer. Touchstones are a valid part of prayer because in the Incarnation "the Word was made flesh, and dwelt among us," as John the Evangelist puts it. The Word continues to be enfleshed in our midst in a myriad of ways.

If we ever meet, ask me about the sword, the cedar blue goblet, and the empty box. That box was once the only touchstone I kept in my oratory for months. There comes a time in our lives when our "incarnational connections" have taken us as far as they can and we must let go and leap into the abyss. As we learn from the Zen Buddhist tradition, the finger pointing to the moon is not the moon. John of the Cross says: "Do not send me any more messengers, they cannot tell me what I must hear." This is what William McNamara calls *the desert experience:* "All the lights go out, idols topple, structures crumble, attachments are sundered, ordinary supports are withdrawn. There is nothing but a veiled God and a promise."

When I lived in monastic community, we always removed our shoes before entering the chapel. I prefer to pray barefoot whenever I can. So did St. Teresa, whose Carmelite Reform is called "discalced" or shoeless. When Moses approached the burning bush, God said, "Remove the sandals from your feet, for the place where you stand is holy ground." Every place God creates is holy ground. But only when we acknowledge one particular place as holy do we recognize them all. This is the paradox of the "concrete universal."

I like to begin my prayer, especially in chapel, with a profound bow from the waist. The quality of that bow determines the quality of my prayer that day, and even the quality of the day. That bow often is my best prayer, as I move my whole body into it as well as heart and mind and soul.

Unlike Buddhist meditation, there is no set posture for Christian prayer. We can stand or sit, either in lotus position or in chairs. We can kneel, a practice not as much in favor as it once was. This is unfortunate, for as British author G.K. Chesterton once wrote: "If we cannot pray, we are gagged. If we cannot kneel, we are in chains." A powerful posture for solitary prayer is prostration: lying face down on the ground in awe, wonder, and humility before the God who created us from nothing. We can keep hands palms up as a sign of our receptivity, rounded and lightly touching as in Buddhist meditation, or clasped together in the more familiar Christian posture. I usually pray with my hands folded, which has always been a natural expression of stillness and reverence for me.

Jesus or Teresa?

WHEN WE READ ABOUT St. Teresa's prayer, we encounter unusual phenomena such as visions and voices. I devote an entire chapter to this "spooky stuff" in my book on Teresa's mystical writings. These experiences have nothing to do with the essence of the mystical life. Classical mysticism considers them "secondary psychophysical phenomena" which appear more frequently in times and temperaments such as Teresa's, which tend toward supernaturalism. If St. Teresa were alive today, she would be aware of the distinction between the psychic and the spiritual and probably express herself differently. I think she would focus more on her inner experience and downplay the secondary and accidental manifestations.

I sometimes find that Christian mysticism is not Christian enough. Instead of looking to Christ and his experience through the scriptures handed down to us, we look too much to "classical" mysticism, which holds up Teresa of Avila as the ideal. I love St. Teresa. She is my patron saint, my sister and my friend, my mentor and my mother, as she is for all Carmelites. I feel closer to her than any other woman I "know." Her mystical writings are a breakthrough in the study of Christian mysticism.

But if we look to Teresa as the classic "mystic" instead of Christ, to *The Interior Castle* instead of the Gospel, to sixteenth-century Spain instead of first-century Palestine, we may be misled. We may become inauthentic, copying the outer behavior of the genuine mystics without an adequate grasp of their inner dispositions. In other words, only Teresa could be a mystic like Teresa, and only you can be a mystic like you.

It is misleading for scholars such as Evelyn Underhill to call Teresa a "mystical genius" without clearly pointing out the supernaturalism of sixteenth-century Spain, acknowledging the power of mind over body, and without pointing to the possibility of Teresa's own neuroses, so evident at the beginning of her religious life. I find it amusing to reflect on what Teresa would have been like if John of the Cross had been her spiritual guide for a longer period, or another woman, or Zorba, our old English sheepdog in Nova Scotia, who really taught me how to pray. Dom John Chapman, an English Benedictine from the last century, believed Teresa was helped more by her bad spiritual advisors than her visions, because suffering is more purifying and conducive to spiritual growth than the enjoyment of unusual experiences.

If we are to be genuine Christian mystics, our mysticism must be more Christocentric and grounded in the Gospels. No one would be more in favor of this than Teresa herself, since she strongly believed that "all our troubles come from not keeping our eyes on Christ."

Authenticity and Intercession

How can we tell whether or not our prayer is real? Authenticity does not depend on feelings, psychophysical experiences, lofty thoughts, noble words, or shifts in consciousness. Our consciousness may indeed enjoy an altered state, but is it elevated? Jesus gives us the acid test of authenticity with a simple question: "What kind of lover are you?" After prayer, are we more considerate, thoughtful, and compassionate? If we continue to be unkind, harshly critical, and unloving, our so-called "prayer" is a sham. Whatever we have been doing may fascinate us, but it cannot be called genuine prayer.

The key to authentic prayer is openness. We must let go of any expectation and cultivate a spirit of expectancy. We must remain empty, like the Virgin Mary's womb, and wait to be impregnated however God sees fit. *"Fiat,* be it done unto me," we pray with the Lady. As we learn from Teresa, prayer is not always tranquil but sometimes tumultuous. Serenity is an important aspect of some prayer, but not all. Sometimes prayer is full of worry, sorrow, and existential anxiety; sometimes full of laughter and joy. We may be still or restlessly pace the floor, arguing with God like Job on his dungheap or struggling with God like Jacob wrestling the angel, as a result of our love-wounds and painful concern for the world.

Christian prayer often takes a form we call "intercession." This experience is sometimes banalized, reduced to telling God what should happen, as if the Almighty didn't know: "Take care of Aunt Sarah during her heart surgery." "Bring peace to the Middle East." "Feed starving Africa." Genuine intercessory prayer cannot be *hortatory* unless it is first *saltatory* (from the Latin *saltere,* to leap). Before we can *exhort* God, we must *leap* into the breach. We must put our bodies on the line and not merely mouth puerile petitions. Our whole being must be behind them. We must feel the hunger, the ravages of war, and Aunt Sarah's anxiety before her operation.

St. Teresa believed in the power of intercessory prayer. She compared it to giving alms. Using another graphic image, she described the sufferer bound to a post, with his hands fastened behind his back by a strong chain. Intercessory prayer loosens the chains. She laughed at the pettiness of some prayer intentions for health, wealth, and money. Although she prayed for these if people asked her, she openly confessed: "I don't think the Lord ever hears me when I pray for these things." In *The Way of Perfection* she insisted that our concerns be global and broad-minded: "The world is all in flames... are we to waste time asking for things... that have little importance?"

When Christian prayer is authentic, the flaming world is always present. This is also true of authentic Buddhist meditation. In Zen practice, the positioning of the hands draws in the universe. The Tibetan practice of *tonglen* is very much like Christian intercession. The practitioner takes in the world's negativity on the in-breath and breathes out love and compassion.

This leads us to the sixth and final stage of prayer, *operatio* or overflowing action. Genuine prayer does not result in feverish activism, compulsive, egotistical, and self-propelled.

It results in Spirit-led enlightened action as an overflow of contemplation, since *action without contemplation is blind.*

Our prayer cannot be a cozy affair between God and me, but must bear fruit for the sake of others. The movement from bed-chamber ecstasy to the ecstasy of service is critical. It is poignant in the life of St. Catherine of Siena. As she grew, Christ did not enter the intimacy of her love-chamber but stood outside her door and beckoned to her, saying: "The service you cannot do me you must render your neighbors." A similar experience galvanized St. Teresa into action for the last laborious years of her life, thrusting her far from the solitude and silence of her monastery cell onto the highways and by-ways of Spain.

This is conveyed in the Buddhist tradition through a series of ox-herding pictures and poems which depict progressive steps in the process of awakening. The last sequence is called "Into the marketplace with empty hands." It was added to the original drawings by the Chinese master Kakuan in the twelfth century and concludes: "Barefooted and naked of breast, I mingle with the people of the world." John the Evangelist challenges East and West alike: "One who has no love for the brother he has seen cannot love the God he has not seen."

CONVERSATION SIX
Celebrating Fast and Feast

A GROUP OF WOMEN walked into the kitchen and found St. Teresa voraciously devouring a roasted partridge. "What are you doing?" they asked, astonished and scandalized. "I'm eating a partridge," Teresa replied. "When I fast, I fast. And when I eat partridge, I eat partridge!" Then she resumed eating with gusto!

This popular story from Teresian lore illustrates the balance between fast and feast, discipline and wildness, asceticism and mysticism. In his sermons on The Song of Songs, St. Bernard says we first kiss the feet of Jesus, then his hands, and only then his mouth. In this progression, Bernard describes the preliminary steps we take before we grow into the intimacy of spousal prayer. The ecstatic wildness of union is usually preceded by disciplined stages traditionally called purgation and illumination. As contemporary poet Richard Wilbur wrote, we must be like St. Teresa, "And lock the O of ecstasy within/ The tempered consonants of discipline."

At its best, Christian spirituality has always emphasized the unity of the ascetical-mystical life. According to William McNamara: "There are positive and negative sides to the spiritual life, times to resist and times to yield, times to gain control and times to let go, a world to deny and a world to affirm. Those who pull off the human adventure, who reconcile the yes and the no, the yin and the yang, are disciplined wild men and women."

Mysticism is the fulfillment of human desire. Intelligent asceticism is the means toward that end, a passionate preparation for Divine Union. This is at once union with God, unity within ourselves, communion among all human persons, and oneness with all that is: animal, vegetable, and mineral.

Asceticism is best understood when we look at its Greek root *askesis,* a strong word which means "training." Through our asceticism, we train ourselves the way a soldier trains for war or an athlete for a contest. Both military combat and the athletic contest are biblical metaphors for the life of the Spirit. "Blessed be the Lord, my rock, who trains my hands for battle, my fingers for war," we pray in Psalm 143. St. Paul describes the Christian life both in terms of fighting and running a race. So does St. Teresa.

The Warrior Spirit

TERESA WAS A CRUSTY OLD WARRIOR, covered with scars from the wounds of war, still glorying in battle; a seasoned explorer of the spirit, fresh with tales from the wild frontier; and a noble knight errant, on a perennial chivalrous quest for the Holy Grail.

Avila was called "the City of Knights." Its narrow winding streets were filled with the dark stone houses of a gallant society that thrived on superhuman exploits. The high arts of chivalry held Avila in its prime. But standing armies and mechanized guns had rendered knighthood superfluous by Teresa's time. The sword at her father's side was simply part of his gentlemanly attire. Yet the spirit of chivalry lived in the heart of Spain and profoundly in Teresa.

As a young girl, Teresa shared her mother's passion for reading chivalric tales. Though she felt guilty deceiving her disapproving father, she was not happy unless she had the latest tale of adventurous quests, dangerous journeys, and romantic love affairs between knights and their ladies. *The Quest of the Holy Grail* delighted Teresa most, with Sir Galahad, son of Lancelot of the Lake, entering heaven wrapped in gold. Teresa and her brother Rodrigo even wrote a story together, called *The Knight of Avila*. This has not been preserved, but Teresa's relatives and friends said it was unusually penetrating for such a young girl.

Although Teresa later regretted wasting time on these chivalrous tales, it seems they were not merely diversion for her, but formed her awakening imagination as much as the pious stories of the saints her father shared. The spirit of chivalry meant honor, grandeur, heroism, and self-sacrifice. In many ways, the chivalric code required behavior very similar to the saint's. The true knight was called to be humble in bearing and courteous in speech, to speak nothing but truth, to do no harm to any creature, and to die rather than run away. No wonder Teresa frequently used imagery taken from the world of the knightly warrior.

This life is war, she declared, referring to ascetical combat and our struggle against *interior* "enemies." We are called to be "true knights of Jesus Christ," "good cavaliers, who desire to serve their king," soldiers eager to fight valiantly, ready for any duty the captain commands. Teresa even describes good friendship in terms of making war together as comrades-in-arms.

We fight for Christ's sake, Christ, whom Teresa calls Knight, Conqueror, Captain, and "Warrior strong." Even when speaking of her Beloved in tender terms, she cannot resist martial imagery and titles him the "Commander-in-Chief of love," who has begun "this war of love!" We must fight out of love for this Beloved, never weary or seeking rest, but embracing persecution and suffering bravely.

Christ is both our guide through the war of this life and "the reward for our warring." In one of her poems, Teresa urges us to risk our lives and follow Christ's banner, exclaiming, "Oh fortunate this war!" We must suffer combat to defend our King, for "few are the vassals remaining with him."

The enemy is always at our doorstep because we are our own worst enemy. Teresa courageously rallies us to *spiritual warfare* not only against the "powers of darkness," but against ourselves. Our "sinfulness" is treachery against the King. The more we grow in contemplation, the greater the battle, especially against the danger of praise.

Our weapons are patience, penance, and the cross. Our banner is Christ, our heraldry his five wounds. Our coat of arms bears the insignia of poverty: in housing, clothing, words, and most of all in thought. We must "stand our ground with a sword in the hand of our thoughts," for the ascetical-mystical life is not only matrimonial but militant, not only wedding but warring.

Some people consider ascetical combat nonsense and the mystical life an illusion or a luxury. Some even call it an irresponsible escape from pressing world problems. But an authentic ascetical-mystical life is not isolated. It is eminently practical: the source of realistic and responsible contemplative action in society, giving hope for the future of our endangered planet.

The true contemplative is capable of truly effective action: social, political, educational, even economic. *Action without contemplation is blind.* The true mystic takes a long loving look at The Real and ends up seeing things as they really are. Genuine contemplative persons, centers, and movements are agents of social change and cultural transformation on both individual and global levels. History provides examples of effective contemplatives in action: Confucius, Lao-Tzu, Sir Thomas More, Mahatma Gandhi, Dag Hammarskjold, Dorothy Day, Mother Teresa. As in previous ages throughout history, the renewal of Western civilization today may depend upon the vitality of our ascetical practice and mystical experience.

Healthy Guidelines

AS WE CONSIDER THE ROLE asceticism plays in our lives to prepare us for spousal prayer and global renewal, here are some essential guidelines. Asceticism is more about transformation than renunciation. Our goal is positive and not punitive. We do not set out to punish our "bad" bodies but purify our inherently good ones. For many centuries, Christians have not given the body the attention it deserves. Suspicion and neglect of the body are great defects in traditional Christianity. This is perplexing, since it diametrically opposes the original Christian teaching and the spirit of Jesus and his robust disciples.

In Hebrew, there are no separate words for "body" and "soul." The Hebrew phrases we often mistranslate dualistically as "body" and "soul" or as "flesh" and "spirit" really mean the whole living person or the whole person deadened or dispirited. Where is the spirit, the soul, the divine image in us? The soul is in our eyes and ears and mouth. The soul is in our hands and feet. The soul is between our legs and in our blood and bones and bowels. This is why the whole human body-person, and the body of the planet, is sacred.

The "Good News" of the Gospel is wholeness, oneness, and unity: "The Word was made flesh, and dwelt among us." (I keep repeating this insight.) This is the Incarnation we celebrate at Christmas. (I wish we'd call the feast Incarnation instead of Christmas, which has so many secular overtones and obscures the deeper mystical significance.)

Throughout history, misguided Christians have crudely separated matter from spirit, body from soul, and earth from heaven, as though one were evil and the other good. It is important to remember that this tendency—whether we call it Manichean, Jansenist, or Docetist—has always been questioned by the Church. At her best, Mother Church has preserved the genuine spirit of Jesus, expressed so beautifully by William McNamara in his first book, *The Art of Being Human*: "Ever since the Incarnation, no one is permitted to scorn or disregard anything human or natural," including the human body and the body of the planet.

In a later study, McNamara goes even further: "The spiritual is not necessarily superior to the material. The material is spiritual." This follows the profound insight of French Jesuit Pierre Teilhard de Chardin, one of my great heroes, who emphasized the spiritual power of matter. If we had grasped the wisdom of this Incarnational insight sooner, we would not have punished our human bodies so badly or damaged the body of the earth so carelessly.

It is important to focus on the positive role of the body, the earth, and the material in Christian spirituality to offset the suspicion of them that has historically characterized our tradition. But we must also be realistic and enlightened in our approach to asceticism. We would be naive if we did not also admit the negative dimension and confess that we experience the body as an obstacle to the spirit as well as a vehicle of the spirit. "The soul loves the body," said Meister Eckhart. But it is equally true to recognize with St. Augustine: "The soul makes war with the body." Or as St. Paul understood so painfully: "I fail to carry out the things I want to do, and I find myself doing the very things I hate."

Any healthy spirituality takes into account our "original sin," whatever we mean by that term. Whatever happened in the Garden of Eden, that is, "in the beginning," something went awry. Genesis tells us that Adam and Eve disobeyed God and ate the apple. Jesus explains that weeds were sown among the wheat. C.S. Lewis says that an evil witch invaded the garden. Jacques Maritain calls this life a "crucified paradise." The Buddhists call it "the wheel of samsara." Each case acknowledges some "bentness" or brokenness in the human person and our need for liberation.

Asceticism is part of our path towards this personal and global liberation.

Natural and Organic

HEALTHY ASCETICISM is natural and organic, not arbitrary or artificial. It grows out of our natural situation and relates specifically to the problem at hand. If we are proud and ambitious and tend to belittle our friends in order to accentuate our self-importance, then it will do no good to wear a hair shirt. It is far more effective to remain quiet about our own accomplishments and instead praise those of others. As Teresa says, "This is true union with [God's] will, and if you see a person praised, the Lord wants you to be much happier than if you yourself were being praised." If we are gluttonous and greedy at supper and grab for food, neglecting to notice the beauty of the meal, ignoring conversation and fellowship around the table, then it will do little good to sing a penitential psalm in Latin and flagellate ourselves every Friday. Far better to serve ourselves last, to wait some time before eating in order to thank those who prepared the meal and comment on its lovely appearance, making sincere and concerned conversation with the family and friends around us.

In our ascetical efforts, it's usually better to avoid extreme measures. William McNamara cautions us against "strongman acts" and Thomas Merton counsels against "spiritual gymnastics." Any ascetical practice should be characterized by sanity, sensitivity, and common sense. A systematic ascetical "program" may be initially helpful but may become defeating because it can lead to pride, self-righteousness, and rigidity. It is far healthier to let life itself become our asceticism. The greatest and most beneficial asceticism is our willing response to whatever life requires of us: not what we want or even think we need, but what life demands.

St. Thérèse of Lisieux, the nineteenth-century follower of Teresa of Avila, is a good ascetical model. As Ida Gorres wrote about her in *The Hidden Face:* "Life itself was her cross, not one or another event in it.... she suffered life as simple and childlike folk must, suffered the permanence and inescapability of its demands." Like Thérèse, instead of trying to escape what life asks of us, it's more helpful to embrace whatever demands life makes on our time and energy.

For me this means sometimes suffering the loneliness of my hermitage when I'd rather be out with friends. Or it may mean the opposite: visiting others or going out to give a talk when I'd rather be in the solitude of my hermitage. It may mean answering emails instead of watching a movie. Or working inside on annual Desert Foundation financial reports when I'd rather be out in the sunshine, pruning trees and stacking wood.

You can draw up a list for your own life, depending on your vocation. Perhaps your life demands taking care of a crying baby, loving an indifferent spouse or a cranky member of your community, coping with a co-worker or family member who is particularly unpleasant. Everyone's "life asceticism" is unique. But the response required is the same for each of us: patience, humility, and creative fidelity.

Ten Spiritual Practices

It's best to respond to the natural, organic, and enlightened *askesis* life offers us. But sometimes we need to engage in a more intentional effort. This will vary, according to the uniqueness of each individual. The following practices seem universal.

1. Commitment

Mystical experience does not occur without a serious commitment to keep growing. St. Teresa urges us to "strive and strive and strive. We are made for nothing else." St. John of the Cross insists that not to move forward is to move backwards. William McNamara defines Christian mysticism in terms of "persevering forward movement" and writes:

> *Mystical experience is far more like learning to walk than learning to fly. An isolated peak human experience is more like the periodic refreshment of a vacation than like the processive daily task of a vocation. Peak experiences are those occasional mountain-top views that encourage us to press on toward the end, to the mystery at the end of the journey, glimpsed and foreshadowed along the way. The daily pressure of the Spirit, the persevering forward movement, the whole experience of life along the way, on the heights or in the hollows—this, and not the sporadic peak experience, is the essence of mystical life.*

We don't move forward and grow when we succumb to the "pilgrim's temptation" and stop along the way. We become settlers instead of pioneers and pilgrims of the Absolute. Seduced by the apparent security and comfort of bourgeois existence, we compromise and become complacent. We settle for what is merely "OK" or "pretty good," rather than aiming for the highest and the best. Instead of really living and growing, which requires a kind of dying, we merely eke out a self-protected quasi-existence. We get stuck on this level. Teresa explains that we won't move out of this lower realm unless we go "mad," take risks and embrace a "holy insecurity," full of *holy daring.*

2. Self-knowledge

"Knowing ourselves is something so important," Teresa says, "that I wouldn't want any relaxation ever in this regard, however high you may have climbed.... For never, however exalted the soul may be, is anything else more fitting than self-knowledge... without it everything goes wrong." As she develops this teaching later in *The Interior Castle,* Teresa insists even more dramatically that "all our trials and disturbances come from our not understanding ourselves."

We desperately need self-understanding. What motivates us in the depths of our being? Why do we do what we do? Who are we? What are our real strengths and weaknesses? How can we expose our weaknesses courageously and break ourselves open to the healing transformative power of the Divine? We come to know ourselves through meditation and prayer, through our relationships in family and community, through mentoring or spiritual guidance, that process the Celtic tradition calls "soul-friending."

3. Accountability

A soul-friend keeps us honest and accountable. Teresa insists that we all need good counsel. According to St. Bernard, when we are guided merely by our own light, we follow the guidance of a fool! We need someone outside ourselves to tell us the truth, to challenge and confront, even to shatter us. Our pride despises or refuses correction. We need soul-friends and mentors to help us. We need to be open to family, friends, and co-workers as instruments of our deepening self-knowledge.

The people around us are not part of our lives by accident. As John of the Cross teaches, they are "craftsmen placed there by God to mortify you by working and chiseling at you. Some will chisel with words, telling you what you would rather not hear; others by deed, doing against you what you would rather not endure; others by their temperament, being in their person and in their actions a bother and annoyance to you; and others by their thoughts, neither esteeming nor feeling love for you."

It's easy to find the "chiselers" in our lives, but not easy to find good soul-friends. In the absence of "official" guidance, we should never underestimate the help we receive from books, family and friends, or from our own prayer. Psychological counseling is also a good aid in the ascetical-mystical life but should never be mistaken for spiritual direction. Nor should spiritual direction take the place of psychological work. I know spiritual directors who say their clients really need therapy and therapists who say their clients really need spiritual guidance.

The Roman Catholic practice of confession is really an act of accountability, elevated to the level of sacrament. It has its counterpart in other traditions, though less formally. This requires a better understanding of what we mean by the old concept of "sin." I was healthily taught that "sin" is being off-target or missing the mark. Bede Griffiths, the Benedictine monk who started a Christian ashram in India, calls it the "consent to unreality, the willing acceptance of an illusion."

It's good to acknowledge the psychological scars which affect our human behavior, but we also need to assume responsibility for our actions and explore the root causes of our inhuman behavior. When we admit our own personal mistakes, we take responsibility for the part we play in hurting others and the human family, a first step towards healing.

4. Friendship

Teresa was warm and affectionate and had an extraordinary gift for friendship. I'd love to write another book just about Teresa and her friends: men and women, family and benefactors, confessors and advisors, friars and nuns, nobles, wealthy businessmen and poor people, sinners and saints. Teresa's 450 extant letters are only a fraction of the number she wrote over her lifetime. She wrote these 450 letters (longhand!) to over 100 different people and mentions almost 800 other friends and acquaintances! Can you image what she would do today with Facebook and other social media?

Spiritual teachers in Teresa's day downplayed the role of spiritual friendship. Her good friend, St. Peter of Alcántara, for example, did not look at a woman for many years, and kept his eyes downcast in his Franciscan monastery, so he only knew his brothers by their voices! But Teresa was a born lover and friend and gives us a remarkable portrait of the primacy of friendship along the spiritual path. "Since spiritual friendship is so extremely important," she wrote at the beginning of her *Life,* "I don't know how to urge it enough."

5. *Simplicity*

It's easy to clutter our lives with too many consumer goods: clothes, cars, gadgets of every kind, wasting too much food and too much energy. Simplifying our lives on every level and developing the habit of frugality is not a once-in-a-lifetime challenge but an ongoing process because of our pack-rat tendency to accumulate "stuff." The beginning of Lent, Advent, and the New Year, even birthdays, are particularly powerful moments to reassess, slim down, and get rid of any excess baggage that bogs us down and holds us back.

Simplicity of life implies some degree of poverty appropriate to our state in life. Teresa did not equate poverty with austerity or destitution. When she took the initial steps to found her first monastery, she wanted it endowed with an income. She feared that poverty would cause distraction and wanted her women freed from financial worry. "For when necessities are lacking," she wisely observed, "many troubles arise." But Teresa also realized that the ownership of property creates many cares as well.

Underlying Teresa's financial astuteness, we find a powerful poverty of spirit and abandonment to what Christians call Divine Providence. "It is not money that will sustain us," she wrote, "but faith, perfection, and trust in God alone." She lauded the freedom of the poor who don't need to kowtow to anyone and never have to wonder whether their "friends" love them or their money. The slavery of riches and the mastery of poverty is one of her impassioned themes

The poverty of a Carmelite monastery is not the poverty of a suburban household. But the same principles apply. Are we ravenous consumers, greedily accumulating more and more, often to hide our inner emptiness, cluttering our houses with junk and the planet with garbage? Or are we reverent contemplatives, walking lightly on the earth, using only what we need, taking nothing for granted, and gratefully appreciating every little thing?

Material poverty is better understood in the context of poverty of spirit. Teresa uses the classical term and calls this detachment. This practice, which Buddhists often call non-attachment, leads to freedom of spirit, simplicity, no-fuss, a light touch, liberation from the attachments, addictions, and fixations that enslave us.

To eliminate grasping, craving, and compulsiveness from our lives, we need to be detached from "creature comforts," worldly vanities, reputation, inordinate preoccupation with health or wealth, and the unhealthy attachments to friends and family that today we call "enmeshment" or "codependency." Teresa's list is not complete. We can all draw up our own lists, perhaps adding attachment or addiction to drugs, alcohol, sex, food, work, success, even technology.

Detachment is a fundamental spiritual discipline and a major factor in our enjoyment of God in spousal prayer. True humility enters in here as well, because, Teresa says, the virtue of humility and the virtue of detachment are inseparable sisters.

6. Rule of Life

We need to eliminate not only the clutter in our houses but the clutter in our hours and reorder our priorities. We may be caught up in peripheral activities that have little to do with what we consider most meaningful in life, what Jesus called "the one thing necessary." Ordering our priorities helps us give our time, talent, and energy to what we value most: celebrating family, friends, and community through leisure and play; celebrating God through prayer and liturgy; celebrating the earth through enjoyment of birds and trees, stars and flowers.

The monastic expression for ordering priorities by ordering the hours of the day is *horarium* or "rule of life." A rule of life improves the quality of our life so that we don't get dragged through the day, controlled by inconsequential external circumstances.

Teresa wrote a rule for her nuns. Whether we are monks in the traditional sense or "new monastics" in the world, we can benefit from Teresa's monastic *Constitutions*. Teresa gives practical advice about how to live our lives in order to make them sane, celebrative, and conducive to spousal prayer, spiritual growth, and service. She emphasizes the importance of silence, reading, regular times and places for prayer, getting up early, accountability, simple food, and universal love. She recommends a daily *examen* to help correct our greatest shortcomings, distinguishes between fruitful and frivolous conversation, and warns us to be careful of excessive comfort.

In our frenzied world of timetables and deadlines, it would help never to be given work with a time limit. Teresa thought this was essential for contemplative life. When buying something, should we follow her no-fuss admonition and "not engage in haggling and bargaining over the price, but after discussing the cost twice... either take the item or leave it?" We should probably ignore Teresa's advice on straw-filled sacks for mattresses, "taking the discipline," and never wearing colors or sheepskins, but it may be beneficial to get rid of our mirrors!

7. Vigilance

We tend to overrate ourselves and our progress. We become smug and inappropriately self-reliant. We get sloppy, lose our attention, and relax our efforts. Teresa calls this presumption a "pestilence" and warns us to be careful about the little things because "little by little, through small things, irremediable harm is done." In our overconfidence, we begin to neglect small but important practices. We sleep late instead of getting up early to pray. We surf the web instead of reading. We accept too many superficial social invitations and lose our spirit of recollection. Instead of challenging ourselves and stretching our limits, we pamper and protect ourselves. We may have so much self-love and so little trust in God that we seek satisfaction in comfortable living. Teresa scolds us: "And yet in our judgment we presume that we are spiritual!"

8. Fasting

We are particularly self-indulgent with food. We eat too much in general and too much of the wrong food. We waste food while others go hungry and become blind to our irresponsibility because our sensitivities are dulled precisely by our overeating and our lack of reading, prayer, and contemplative stillness. We need to eat less, more simply, and lower down on the food chain. But we need to fast from more than food. We need to fast from too much comfort and toughen up. We need to fast from too much work and cultivate the contemplative spirit of celebration and play. We need to fast from too much talk, foster the spirit of silence and read more, but discriminately. Just as it is physically unhealthy to feed the body with junk-food, it is mentally unhealthy to feed the mind with junk-reading. We cannot afford to read what is merely good, but only the very best.

9. Solitude

We need to fast from too much togetherness and enjoy more solitude. Solitude is not only for monks, nuns, and hermits but for everyone, married people with families included.

Blaise Pascal, the seventeenth-century French genius in both science and spirituality, said: "All our troubles in life come because we refuse to sit quietly for a while each day in our rooms." According to Edward Ford, husband and father of eight, who helps spouses become better friends to one another: "Of all the things you can do by yourself... getting a job, going to school, working for charity—creative solitude on a daily or semi-daily basis (in brief, endurable chunks) will be the most important." Teresa puts it more poetically:

There is no need to go to heaven in order to speak with [the Beloved].... Nor is there any need to shout. However softly we speak, He is near enough to hear us. Neither is there any need for wings to go to find Him. All one need do is go into solitude and look at Him within oneself, and not turn away from so good a Guest.

Paradoxically, when we are solitary, we best express our solidarity with the entire universe. According to William McNamara:

Solitude is a creative protest against the euphoric or chaotic togetherness that stamps our way of life in the modern world. But it is also the highest and most apt expression of our solidarity with the whole human race, with the whole of creation. The more solitary we are, the more we are divinely endowed and psychologically equipped to enter into a significantly profound relationship with all levels of life—animal, vegetable and mineral as well as human.

117

10. Humility

The spiritual life is built on humility. Teresa does not mince words here. If there is no growth in humility, "Everything is going to be ruined." She also uses comforting imagery in her descriptions of this foundational virtue: Humility is an ointment for our wounds. If we are humble, an indispensable requirement for spousal prayer, the surgeon, who is our Beloved, will come to heal us.

Teresa's own life is a model of humility. "I could be mistaken," she admits over and over again in her writings. "Perhaps I don't know what I'm talking about." She begs pardon for speaking boldly of sublime matters. She implores those who edit her work to cross out whatever is inappropriate, tear it up, or burn it. She even hopes they will get a good laugh out of her foolishness!

In the midst of the *Life*, she begs her censor not to cut out anything about her failings because they tell the story of God's mercy. In the prologue to *The Interior Castle*, she explains that she writes only for her sisters because it's "nonsense" to think that anything she says could matter to anyone else. Through humility we clearly perceive how great God is and how helpless we often are. She said, "[I] know what You can do and what I can do."

Teresa also distinguishes between true and false humility. As we get to know ourselves, we may become discouraged. But this distress should be quiet, calm, and full of compunction. Self-knowledge is a merciful gift from God and increases real humility. If we experience excessive distress, anger, agitation, and frustration, this is a sign of false humility, wounded pride, and egotism. We may grieve over our shortcomings, but what matters more is the unfathomable mercy of God. When we are humble, we take God so seriously that we take everything else, especially ourselves, light-heartedly.

Teresa teaches that humility is walking in truth: the truth of who we are and who God is. Since humility is truth, it does not mean thinking little of ourselves, but thinking of ourselves very little. This is a warrior virtue. Humility carries with it a breath of greatness, a jubilant freedom, holy audacity and *holy daring,* the very qualities we need to walk the tightrope.

At the feet of St. Teresa, Avila, 1990

CONCLUSION
Walking the Tightrope

TRUTH IS TWO-EYED, teaching us to hold two seeming contraries in our minds at the same time, "eternally bent over the double abyss," as mystic writer Angela of Foligno expressed it. "Religion has its very life in what are paradoxes and contradictions in the eye of reason," wrote John Henry Newman, controversial British convert to Roman Catholicism in the nineteenth century. "Such seeming contradictions," he also wrote, "arise from the want of depth in our minds to master the whole truth. We have not eyes keen enough to follow out the lines of God's providence and will, which meet at length though at first sight they seem parallel."

Teresa knew how to balance life's apparent inconsistencies. She taught us to pray, "Let nothing disturb you," yet experienced distress, anger, and heartbreak. She advised us to sleep no less than six hours each day, but stayed up through the night writing letters. Tenderly loving her family, she was often glad to be far away from them. She withdrew into deep silence and solitude, then encouraged high times and high jinks. She ascetically chided her followers for pampering their bodies but ordered them to stop walking barefoot in the snow and to use good sheets and table linens.

There is no escape from dualism if we limit ourselves to sense perception or discursive thought. According to Nicolas of Cusa, fifteenth-century philosopher and bishop, "Only in the mystical experience is the dilemma of duality resolved. For to the mystic is given the unifying vision of the One in the All and the All in the One.... It is only through the coincidence or reconciliation of polar opposites that God is found."

If we are not mystical, we opt for only one end of the spectrum and end up bland and mediocre. We do not reveal our greatness by being at one extremity or the other, but rather by touching both at once, said Blaise Pascal in his passion. Energy, creativity, and mystical experience lie in the dynamic interplay between seemingly opposing polar forces.

St. Teresa, the wild woman of Avila, teaches us to live life in its total polarity: agony and ecstasy, warring and wedding, madness and reason, masculine and feminine, action and contemplation, discipline and wildness, fast and feast. It takes *holy daring*, a muscular personality, and more than a touch of madness to suffer the creative tension of the mystic way, to risk living the paradox, to adventure far enough to leave perplexing polarities behind and integrate them into a higher synthesis.

Life is not either-or but both-and. We need to be quick-change artists and multiple amphibians, at home in many worlds. We need Teresa's holistic spirituality of "harmony in tension." This harmony is not won easily. The tension is both crucifying and creative. The world's great balancing acts come to mind: acrobats and dancers, jugglers and mimes, trapeze artists and tightrope walkers.

Philippe Petit is the astonishing Frenchman who walked the high wire between the two towers of Notre Dame Cathedral in Paris in 1971, between the twin towers of New York's World Trade Center three years later in 1974. Petit gives us deep insights into the miracle of tension we must live to be integrated and whole. His descriptions of tightrope walking sound like St. Teresa to me.

Petit is full of *duende* and feels like a matador facing a bull who dreams of tearing him to pieces or like a slave "who must march or die." "It is madness," he says of the Trade Center exploit: "It is too painful." He is "cold with fear," yet experiences a "revolution of happiness." He approaches the wire wild with excitement, but with disciplined eyes and feet: "I know that I will not be able to go backward. I am going to launch myself into a part of my life and enjoy with pleasure and terror that role which I have chosen." Fighting against the wind and the swaying of the wire, he thinks: "This immense gulf has the power to make me lose my head if I allow myself, even for a single second, to give up the fight. My head is ready to break into pieces. My legs are ready to tremble. My body is perhaps ready to give up. But not I. Not ever."

This sounds like St. Teresa meditating on the crucified Christ. Or like Jesus from the cross, one of the world's greatest balancing acts, a miracle of tension that becomes a miracle of balance. Crucifixion does not require a rope or a steel wire stretched across a gaping chasm, but the sinews of the God-Man's flesh, stretched beyond the breaking point in a breakdown of human limitation that breaks through into divine impossibility: Easter out of Good Friday, light out of darkness, life out of death. "You kill," marveled St. Teresa, "leaving me with more life."

Those who view the cross from the outside see it as an obstacle, a stumbling block, deadly, illogical, and insane. Those who are initiated into its mystery through pain and suffering see the cross as the power and wisdom of God: "For God's foolishness is wiser than human wisdom, and God's weakness is stronger than human strength," wrote St. Paul.

The cross is the ultimate Christian *koan.* Like the ancient *koans,* or riddles, used by generations of Zen masters, the mystery of the cross shocks us out of our mental ruts and our conventional, routine piety. William McNamara describes it eloquently: "We experience disaster on a certain theological and conceptual level and the simultaneous or subsequent awakening of our mythopoeic and existential awareness. And we are never quite the same again." Suzuki Roshi called it "Zen mind, beginner's mind." Christians may call it "resurrection mind" and speak of putting on the mind of Christ. In one of his poems, Pope St. John Paul II marvels at the mystery of this rite of passage when the path we ordinarily know reverses direction:

> *From life to pass into death*
> *—this is our experience,*
> *this is what we see.*
> *Through death*
> *to pass into life—*
> *This is the mystery.*

This is why we Christians wear the cross around our necks, hang it on our walls, and sign ourselves with it at prayer. This is why we image and re-image it in clay and wood, paint, glass, and stone, why we write poetry and music and sing about it, why we bow low before it. As G.K. Chesterton put it, when we bow down in adoration before Mystery, "the whole world turns upside right."

What seems upside down for those who are not on the mystical path seems upside right to St. Teresa, who teaches us to pray with every fiber of our being bent over the double abyss:

> *Give me death, give me life,*
> *Health or sickness,*
> *Honor or shame,*
> *War or swelling peace,*
> *Weakness or full strength,*
> *Yes, to these I say,*
> *What do you want of me?*
>
> *Give me wealth or want,*
> *Delight or distress,*
> *Happiness or gloominess,*
> *Heaven or hell,*
> *Sweet life, sun unveiled,*
> *To you I give all.*
> *What do you want of me?*
>
> *Give me, if You will, prayer;*
> *Or let me know dryness,*

An abundance of devotion,
Or if not, then barrenness.
In you alone, Sovereign Majesty,
I find my peace,
What do you want of me?

Give me then wisdom.
Or for love, ignorance,
Years of abundance,
Or hunger and famine.
Darkness or sunlight,
Move me here or there:
What do you want of me?

If you want me to rest,
I desire it for love;
If to labor,
I will die working:
Sweet Love say
Where, how and when.
What do you want of me?...

Yours I am, for You I was born:
What do you want of me?

CHRONOLOGY
OF ST. TERESA'S LIFE

1515   Teresa de Cepeda y Ahumada born in Avila
        on March 28.

1528   Teresa's mother dies.

1535   Teresa enters Calced Carmelite Monastery
        of the Incarnation on November 2.

1539   Seriously ill, returns to her father's home and
        lapses into a coma for four days. Brought
        back to the Incarnation and paralyzed for
        three years.

1554   During Lent, experiences a radical
        conversion before a statue of Christ at the
        pillar.

1556   Receives the grace of spiritual betrothal in May.

1560   Receives the grace of transverberation.
        Begins discussing a new reformed
        "Discalced" monastery.

1562   Finishes first edition of the *Life* in June.
        Secretly founds new monastery of St.
        Joseph's in August. Ordered back to
        Monastery of the Incarnation. Moves back

	to St. Joseph's in December and changes name to Teresa de Jesús.
1563	Writes the *Constitutions* for Discalced Carmelites at St. Joseph's.
1566	Finishes *The Way of Perfection* and writes *Meditations on the Song of Songs.*
1567	Carmelite Prior General authorizes Teresa to found more new Discalced monasteries. First meets John of the Cross on travels to Medina del Campo.
1568	Travels to Malagón and Valladolid. Teaches John of the Cross her way of life in August. John and another friar begin first monastery of Carmelite men in November.
1569	Teresa travels to Toledo and Pastrana. Writes the *Soliloquies.*
1570	Travels to Salamanca.
1571	Travels to Alba de Tormes, reluctantly made Prioress at Monastery of the Incarnation.
1572	John of the Cross becomes chaplain and confessor at Monastery of the Incarnation. Teresa receives the grace of spiritual marriage in November.
1573	Begins writing the *Foundations.*
1574	Travels to Segovia. Princess of Eboli denounces Teresa's *Life* to the Inquisition.

1575	Travels to Beas and Seville. First meets Jerónimo Gracián. Disgruntled nun denounces Teresa to Inquisition in Seville. Struggles with the Calced Carmelites. Ordered to leave Andalucia and retire to one of her Discalced monasteries in Castile.
1576	Arrives in Toledo. Continues writing the *Foundations*. Persecution by the Calced Carmelites intensifies.
1577	Begins writing *The Interior Castle* on June 2. Arrives in Avila in July. Finishes *The Interior Castle* on November 29. John of the Cross imprisoned by the Calced Carmelites on December 3. Teresa falls and breaks her left arm on December 24.
1578	John of the Cross escapes from his Toledo prison in August. Teresa's Discalced nuns and friars placed under the authority of the Calced Carmelites. Most troubled year for Teresa's Reform.
1579	End of persecution by the Calced Carmelites. Teresa travels to Malagón in June.
1580	Travels to Villanueva de la Jara in February and Toledo in March and becomes seriously ill. A papal brief in June allows Teresa's Discalced nuns and friars to separate from the Calced Carmelites. Travels to Valladolid in August and falls seriously ill again. Travels

to Palencia in December.

1581   Discalced Carmelites finally separate from the Calced and confirm their *Constitutions*. Gracián elected first provincial leader in March. Teresa travels to Soria in June.

1582   Teresa leaves Avila for the last time in January and travels to Burgos. Travels to Alba de Tormes. On September 29 goes to bed seriously ill, never to get up again, announces her death. On October 3 makes her last confession and receives the Sacrament of the Dying. Dies on October 4 at age 67. (The Gregorian calendar was introduced that year. The day following Teresa's death became October 15, which eventually became her Feast Day.)

1614   On April 24, Pope Paul V "beatifies" Teresa, the first step towards official canonization.

1622   On March 12, Pope Gregory XV canonizes Teresa with Saints Isidore the Farmer, Ignatius of Loyola, Francis Xavier, and Philip Neri.

1970   On September 27, Pope Paul VI declares Teresa the first woman Doctor of the Church.

TESSA BIELECKI lives in a hermitage in Crestone, Colorado, in the spirit of the Christian Mothers and Fathers of the desert. Co-founder of the Spiritual Life Institute, she was a Carmelite monk and Mother Abbess for almost 40 years, establishing radically experimental monastic communities of men and women in Arizona, Colorado, Nova Scotia, and Ireland. She was also editor-in-chief of *Desert Call*, the quarterly magazine of the community. In 2005, she left SLI to embrace the eremitical life more fully and co-found The Desert Foundation with friend and fellow hermit, Father Dave Denny. The Desert Foundation (www.sandandsky.org) is an informal circle of friends who explore the wisdom of the desert and encourage understanding between the three Abrahamic traditions: Judaism, Christianity and Islam.

Tessa is the author of several critically acclaimed books on Teresa of Avila, including *Teresa of Avila: Mystical Writings*, and *Teresa of Avila: Ecstasy and Common Sense*. She recently recorded *Teresa of Avila: The Book of My Life* for Shambhala Audio and *Wild at Heart: Radical Teachings of the Christian Mystics* for Sounds True. She co-authored a new collection of writings on the Christmas season, *Season of Glad Songs*, with Father Dave Denny, and continues to teach on Christian mysticism and the contemplative life at retreats and workshops around the world.

Printed in the USA
CPSIA information can be obtained
at www.ICGtesting.com
JSHW082350140824
68134JS00020B/1991